THE PASTA
BOOK

THE PASTA

Introduced by Luigi Veronelli

Compiled by Simonetta Lupi Vada

B·O·O·K

ST. MARTIN'S PRESS

Recipes
Simonetta LUPI VADA

Editorial Consultants
Stephen SCHMIDT
Anna Maria MASCHERONI

Photographers
Piero BAGUZZI - Alberto BERTOLDI
Mario MATTEUCCI - Romano VADA

Production Services
STUDIO ASTERISCO, Milan

Copyright © 1985 by Gruppo Editoriale Fabbri S.p.A., Milan

English language text copyright © 1985
by Gruppo Editoriale Fabbri S.p.A., Milan

Printed in Italy by Gruppo Editoriale Fabbri S.p.A., Milan
For information, address
St. Martin's Press, 175 Fifth Avenue,
New York, NY 10010

ISBN 0-312-59796-7

Published in Italy in 1985 by Gruppo Editoriale Fabbri S.p.A.
First published 1985 in the United States by St. Martin's Press,
175 Fifth Avenue, New York, NY 10010

Library of Congress Catalog Card Number: 85-10806

10 9 8 7 6 5 4 3 2 1

SUMMARY

WHEAT AND FLOUR

The wheat
The structure of the wheat kernel
Durum wheat
The milling process
Characteristics of different types of flour

COMMERCIAL PASTA

The production of dried pasta
Nutritional value

HOMEMADE PASTA

The dough
Colored pasta
Stuffed pasta
Some typical regional varieties of pasta
The Mediterranean diet

ADVICE FROM THE EXPERTS

What makes good pasta?
The ten golden rules for cooking pasta
Hints on serving pasta
Sauces for different types of pasta
Can pasta be frozen?

RECIPES

Pasta with ragù (meat sauces)
Pasta with vegetable sauces
Pasta with fish sauces
Pasta with white sauces
Stuffed pasta
Gnocchi
Crêpes

I am a passionate lover of long, twisting, stringy spaghetti, of maccheroni, vermicelli, avemarie, tagliolini, tagliatelle, bucatini (don't stop), and to me a book like this is more, much more than merely an invitation to a feast.

Pasta, often referred to by the universally known name of "spaghetti", is such an "in" thing that it is of interest to everyone, from the least food-conscious to the most sophisticated palates among us. The truth of the matter is: pasta has conquered the world.

The success of pasta is anything but sudden and is not, therefore, just a passing fad. Alexandre Dumas, who was a great connoisseur of Neapolitan culture from his experiences as one of Garibaldi's thousand followers, stated more than a century ago that spaghetti was "a European dish which has travelled with civilization and which, like civilization, is to be found a long way from its cradle".

That is not all: Giuseppe Prezzolini, a professor at Columbia University, New York, in the 1930s, actually stated in his book, *Spaghetti Dinner,* that spaghetti was the American national dish: "Spaghetti was introduced to the United States by Thomas Jefferson along with poplars from Lombardy, Roman architecture and Tuscan wine. He even imported the first spaghetti machine."

As if that were not enough, pasta has in recent years been loudly hailed as possessing the ultimate virtue. As part of the so-called "Mediterranean diet", pasta is good for you. It keeps you healthy and young, and may even have aphrodisiac properties!

And so this book is more than welcome. It contains useful background information on types of wheat and flour, looks into commercially produced and homemade pasta (and thankfully returns, inevitably, to the virtues of the home-

The regions of Italy

made). Detailed instructions are included on how to select and combine the ingredients, prepare and color the dough, roll it out and cut the various pasta shapes.

It is a complete and fascinating book which unravels the mysteries of, for example, stuffed pasta, the many interesting regional variations in pasta shapes, or the feasibility and methods of freezing pasta (so necessary these days). There is valuable, detailed advice on how to cook and serve perfect pasta and which sauce to choose to complement different pasta types.

Then there are the recipes. So many that one could go on almost indefinitely. Because there are thousands of ways of cooking pasta or, to be precise, ways of combining it with different ingredients and sauces. Here you will find all the best recipes as you are taken on a comprehensive and frenetic journey through Italy. Because there is not one place, from the snowy peaks of the Alps to the sun-baked southern coasts, where you are not offered an age-old traditional dish or some new happy invention of the cook: a plateful of steaming pasta, enlivened with different colors and flavors, depending on local custom. Each one of these recipes provides delightful evidence of the versatility of pasta. Try them out, serve them to your family and friends — and don't forget the wine.

On the subject of wine with pasta, I disagree with three authorities: Alberto Denti di Pirajno, Luigi Carnacina and Mario Soldati. Alberto Denti di Pirajno pronounced: "After eating pasta with tomatoes, you should not be so profane as to drink wine; on top of pasta and tomatoes, only water should be drunk." In this instance I support the attitude of the supposedly prejudice-free Venetians when they say: "The best rule is not to follow any rules." To my mind, it is water, not wine, that is sacrilegious with pasta and tomatoes. Luigi Carnacina and Mario Soldati advise against drinking wine with pasta either because this is the rule of grand cuisine or for dietetic reasons (the lipids in the pasta apparently clash with the alcohol in the wine and hamper digestion). That's a lot of nonsense. An eighteenth-century Sicilian proverb very clearly tells us: *"Voi campari anni e anni? Vivi vinu supra li maccaruni."* (Do you want to live to a ripe old age? Then drink wine with macaroni.) Which wine? In my book, there is only one rule that can be applied without exception: the choice of wine is to be governed by the sauce that accompanies the pasta. Pasta, which is practically inedible on its own, bursts with flavor when accompanied by even the simplest of sauces. By which I mean a few tomatoes, cooked and puréed, or just garlic and oil. It stands to reason that it should be the sauce to govern the choice of wine. With a vegetable sauce choose a light white or rosé; with a fish sauce a balanced, dry, white wine; for meat sauces a dry, light, red wine; and to accompany game a dry, full-bodied red wine.

A word of warning: wines should be lighter, younger and fresher than you would choose if you were using the same ingredients — vegetables, fish, meat or game — as dishes in their own right rather than as sauces. The reasons are obvious: the ingredients have been "diluted" to the consistency of a sauce, the final effect is not so rich, and the flavor is further attenuated by the bland taste of the pasta.

The invitation to a feast is now before you. It is up to you, my reader friend and kindred spirit, to accept it and, having become an expert by attentive reading, return the invitation.

WHEAT AND FLOUR

The wheat - Wheat, from which pasta is made, is the most universally cultivated cereal (followed by rice) and is mainly used for human consumption. The history of wheat is closely bound up with the history of mankind. Wheat probably developed accidentally from the crossing of wild grass species. It was first cultivated more than 6,000 years ago in Asia Minor, whence it spread through the Middle East to Egypt and the Mediterranean and subsequently to northern Europe and the countries of the New World (which today represent the major producers and exporters of wheat).

As the cultivation of wheat spread to areas with different climatic and soil conditions, new varieties developed with distinctive structural characteristics adapted to the new conditions. On the basis of these characteristics wheat can be divided into two main groups: the soft-wheats, including the *Triticum vulgare* species, and the hard-wheats which include the species *Triticum durum, Triticum orientale* and *Triticum persicum*.

Soft-wheats are grown in all the countries with a temperate climate and also where there is intensive cultivation. Hard-wheats are grown in Africa, North and South America and the Mediterranean area. One group of hard-wheats, known as durum wheats, is generally considered to be the best for pasta-making.

There are, however, numerous agricultural and commercial varieties within each species and each one has different structural characteristics (for example, the shape of the ear, the length of the kernel, the structure of the endosperm), biological characteristics (such as resistance to adverse atmospheric and climatic conditions, parasites and disease) and qualitative characteristics (chemical composition, suitability for processing and milling).

Through genetic engineering, it has become possible to bring together all the most desirable characteristics of the different species in one single variety. This has improved the structural, biological and qualitative features and increased the productivity of the cereal.

The structure of the wheat kernel - A kernel of wheat is composed of three main parts. The outer covering consists of several layers of fibrous bran. Inside is the germ, or embryo, of the new plant. The bulk (80%) of the kernel consists of the endosperm, the starchy food supply for the new plant. Most flour, apart from whole-wheat and brown flours, is the product of the milled endosperm of the wheat kernel.

Durum wheat - There are several varieties of durum wheat within the larger category of the hard wheats. The wheat grain or kernel is very large, often exceeding $1/2$ inch in length. As the name implies, the endosperm of durum wheat is very hard and is pigmented so that it yields an amber-colored semolina. This color is reflected in the characteristic amber yellow of pasta. Durum wheat is also rich in gluten. Taken together, its properties make for pasta that dries easily and holds together well during cooking. Durum wheat is too hard to be suitable for bread-making. It grows best in arid areas and is cultivated extensively in the Mediterranean, the southern U.S.S.R. and parts of Canada and the U.S.A.

The milling process - Before it is actually milled, the wheat grain is subjected to a series of wet and dry cleaning processes to extract foreign matter such as dust, grit and straw, and also to eliminate unwanted parts of the grain itself such as the husk and spikes. Simultaneously, conditioning processes regulate the extent to which the grain is dried in order to improve the quality and yield of the finished product.

After these operations, the milling process begins. This consists essentially of breaking down the grain and the gradual removal of the outer layers of bran. In the first stage of the milling process the grain is crushed between huge rollers. This produces coarse granules. The bran and germ are then separated off by sifting and winnowing in special cylinders.

The "stripped" endosperm is now a granular meal which is pulverized by further milling and transformed into quality flour. The flour is sifted repeatedly until the required degree of fineness is obtained. In the production of whole-wheat flour the milling process involves the cleaning, breaking up and grinding of the wheat, but the bran and germ are purposely not removed and are present, coarsely ground, in the finished flour. Only flours containing the bran and germ can be termed "whole-wheat" flours.

Flour can also be produced by stone-milling the grain between large millstones. This method goes back to prehistory and is efficient, but most large-scale manufacturers use the more modern roller-milling methods.

Characteristics of different types of flour - Ordinary flour is the product of soft wheats that have been milled to remove the bran and germ. It is a yellowish-white when first milled (the whiteness of commercial flour is the result of subsequent bleaching). It is pleasant to taste and smell and is so fine it is impalpable to the touch. This type of flour is most suitable for making cakes and pastries and has many other culinary uses, for example in sauce making.

"Bread" flour is a combination of flours milled from hard and soft wheats. It is rich in gluten and is therefore good for bread-making. Commercially produced bread is often made from a mixture of soft-wheat and hard-wheat flours.

Whole-wheat flour is coarser than both all-purpose and bread flour and is flecked with brown particles denoting the presence of bran and wheat germ. Because of the fat contained in the germ, this type of flour does not keep as long as the other flours.

For homemade pasta, the best flours are hard-wheat or bread flours, or whole-wheat flour for making whole-wheat pasta. The best commercially produced pasta is always made from milled durum wheat in the form of semolina, that is, coarsely ground meal, rather than more finely ground flour. This is because flour in the granular form of semolina absorbs less water than finer flour and will dry more quickly. Although semolina can be bought in packages for use at home, it is not usually used for homemade pasta. Pasta made at home is, after all, fresh pasta and does not need to have good drying or long-keeping qualities. Bread flour is perfectly satisfactory for homemade pasta.

The different types of flour vary in nutritional content. This is related to the nutrients contained in the various parts of the wheat kernel: the bran, germ and endosperm.

Flour made from endosperm alone will contain about 70% of the protein present in the original grain and some vitamins of the B complex. As a starch food it is predominantly a form of energy. Extra vitamins and iron are often added to flour after milling. However, all-purpose flour contains little dietary fiber. Whole-wheat flour from which nothing has been removed contains all the protein and vitamins originally present in the grain of wheat (apart from a small percentage lost during processing). In addition, the cellulose material in the bran provides a valuable amount of dietary fiber.

COMMERCIAL PASTA

Pasta is obtained from the processing of wheat flour. Its origins are extremely ancient: they go back as far as the Etruscans who are said to have made the first lasagna noodles. The use of pasta spread across Italy from the fourteenth century onwards, and it was at the beginning of the nineteenth century that the first simple pasta machines appeared in Naples. Nowadays, modern technology has made it possible to standardize the production processes, and pasta factories are to be found all over Italy and in other countries too.

Commercial pasta is made from two basic ingredients: flour and water. However, for the end-product to be very good quality, great care must be taken over the choice of the two ingredients and the method of production. The flour should be from hard-wheat semolina, suitably milled and sifted. If the particles of flour are too large, this can cause the formation of white spots in the pasta, due to imperfect hydration. The pasta will tend to crumble and become translucent in appearance. On the other hand, if the particles of flour are too small, this can lead to thermal stress during production and the quality of the product will suffer. The protein-rich part of the flour, known as *gluten*, is very important, as this is the ingredient which makes the pasta cohere. The other ingredient, water, must also be chosen accurately: it is best if the water is medium hard with a low level of sodium, magnesium and chlorine and a very low concentration of iron.

For egg pasta and the so-called "special" pasta, other ingredients are required, as described on page 21.

The production of dried pasta - The flour and the water are combined in a machine called a press which functions continuously: the raw materials are constantly fed into the press which continuously produces pasta. The kneading process follows. This consists of a final kneading of the dough to make it homogeneous and malleable.

The dough is then drawn out and passed through various dies or forms which determine the shape and appearance of the finished product. Some of the shapes obtained from drawing the dough through these dies are: spaghetti, smooth tagliatelle (noodles) and scalloped tagliatelle, farfallette (butterflies or bows), quadrucci (squares), rigatoni (fluted tubes), smooth penne (quills) and fluted penne, lingue di passero (very thin noodles), capelli d'angelo (very thin spaghetti) and many others. Dried pasta shapes are divided into two main categories: *pasta asciutta*, for cooking in water and eating with sauces, and *pasta in brodo*, smaller shapes for cooking in a broth or soup.

In all these types of pasta, the texture of the surface is important. The advantage of commercial pasta is that it absorbs sauces and seasonings better, while the disadvantage is that it does not stand up to cooking so well. After the drawing-out stage, the pasta is in its final shape but still contains about 30% too much water and so will not keep well. The water content has to be reduced to about 12.5% and this process involves various delicate stages on which the final quality of the product depends. The first stage (pre-wrapping) consists of intensive ventilation of the pasta in order to dry the surface and prevent it from sagging and losing its shape. The wrapping follows this first stage and removes a large percentage of the water that still remains in the pasta. Again, this is a critical operation, for drying the pasta too quickly will cause it to lose its shape and crack, while if it is dried out too slowly it will become acid and turn moldy. After a "resting" stage, the purpose of which is to allow any water still present in the pasta to redistribute itself evenly within the product, there are two more drying stages which bring the pasta down to its final level of moisture content. The drying is carried out at a temperature between 113°F and 158°F and takes between 6 and 28 hours depending on the shape. At this point, the pasta needs a "maturing" period during which the product becomes "stable", thus avoiding a drastic change of environment from the place where it is produced, which is suitably air-conditioned, to the temperature outside, which could cause it to deteriorate.

Packaging is the last stage in this series of operations. Pasta is packaged in cellophane packets or cardboard boxes of various shapes and sizes. Up until this point, the pasta is free from contaminants.

Nutritional value - The nutritional properties of pasta come from the high starch (carbohydrate) content (70-75%), the relatively high protein content (11-12%), and the presence of some vitamins and minerals plus a little fiber. The fat content is low (less than 1%). The caloric value of pasta is about 350 calories every 4 ounces, the average portion size. Whole-wheat pasta contains additional protein and approximately 10% by weight of dietary fiber. All types of pasta are quickly digested and assimilated by the body aiding respiration and providing heat and energy. For a balanced meal that will meet all the body's requirements for heat, energy, tissue repair and growth (in the case of children), pasta needs to be combined with protein foods such as meat, poultry, fish or cheese. That is why pasta with a meat sauce, or even with butter and cheese, makes a nutritionally satisfying meal. The versatility of pasta is proved by the huge number of recipes to which pasta lends itself. This, together with its low cost, has made pasta a success all over the world. Today, the "Mediterranean diet", based on pasta as a staple, is engaging the attention of scientists and nutritionists, many of whom suggest that it is the healthiest and most balanced diet there is.

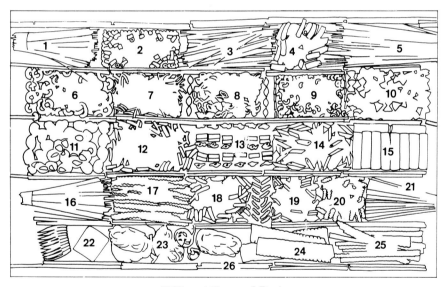

Different Types of Pasta

1 Whole-wheat bucatini - 2 Ditalini, tubetti, maccheroncini - 3 Spaghetti - 4 Maccheroni, maniche di frate - 5 Whole-wheat spaghetti - 6 Creste - 7 Sedanini, gramigna gigante - 8 Lumachine - 9 Sedani ritorti, gobbetti, pipe - 10 Farfalle, galani - 11 Lumaconi, chiocciole - 12 Whole-wheat maccheroni - 13 Marille, maccheroni - 14 Maltagliati, penne - 15 Cannelloni - 16 Green bigoli - 17 Long fusilli - 18 Short fusilli, viti - 19 Green short fusilli, viti, delizie - 20 Reginelle, pappardelle - 21 Trenette, bavette - 22 Lasagne, dollari - 23 Tagliatelline, tagliatelle, fettucce, lasagnette, lagane, laganelle - 24 Pappardelle - 25 Pappardelle, mafaldine - 26 Zite, long maccheroni (as it is called in the South)

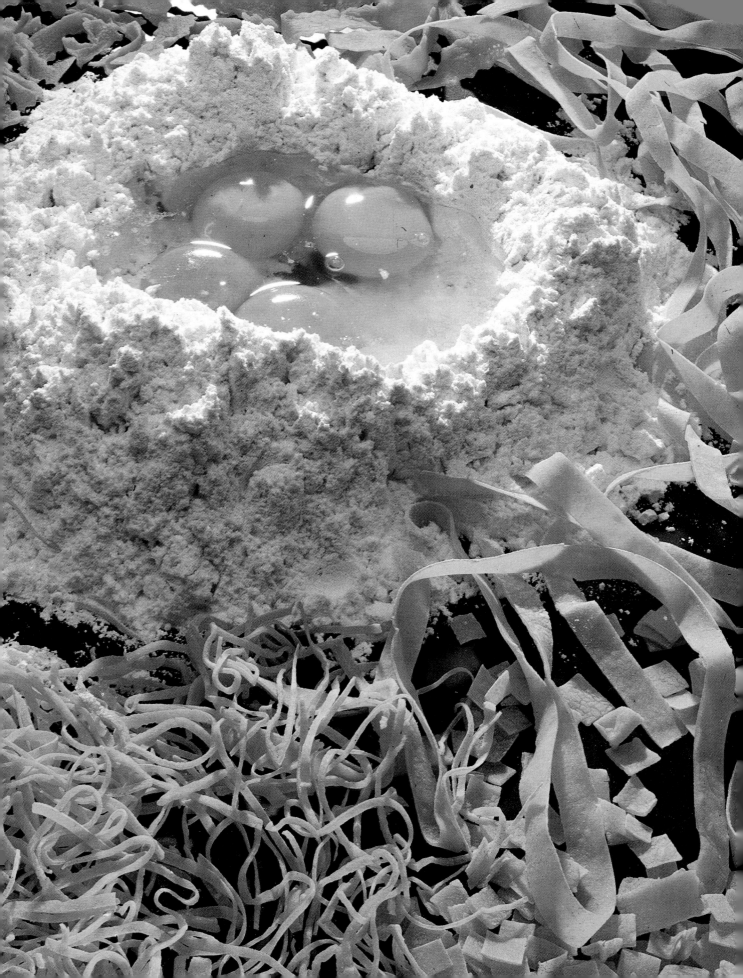

HOMEMADE PASTA

The term *pasta casalinga*, as fresh pasta is called in Italy, generally means pasta made with egg, flour and, sometimes, olive oil. There are other types of pasta made with flour from different kinds of cereal, and mixed only with water.

THE DOUGH

Utensils - To prepare egg pasta the authentic way you need only a few utensils, but they should have specific characteristics. First of all, you need a wooden pastry board, which should be long and wide and perfectly smooth, with no knots. Alternatively, a marble slab may be used, but a wooden board is better as it enables you to stretch the dough into a very thin sheet and the wood absorbs any excess moisture from the dough while the pasta is being kneaded. Another essential piece of equipment is a long wooden rolling pin (traditionally made of cherry wood and as smooth as a looking glass). Its size is also important: about 2 inches in diameter and at least a yard long, so that the dough can be wrapped around it and turned without hanging over the ends of the pin and breaking off.

You also need a fairly short, flexible, metal spatula to lift the dough from the pastry board, a serrated or smooth wooden pastry wheel and a very sharp, wide-bladed knife to cut the dough into various shapes.

Nowadays, the rolling pin has been replaced by either manual or electric pasta machines for stretching the dough. The most recent electric machines enable you to go from the raw-ingredient stage to cutting out the shapes in next to no time. The manual machine is more common because it costs less and is easy to use. It has smooth rollers to stretch the pasta into a sheet and ridged rollers to cut the rolled-out dough into tagliatelle (noodles) and tagliolini (thin noodles). The sheet of dough can be made even finer by adjusting the distance between the two smooth rollers. The rollers are turned by means of a handle.

The electric pasta machine works in the same way but is operated by a motor. With an electric pasta machine, all you have to do is put the ingredients (following the instruction booklet or recipe for quantities) into the appropriate containers, close the lid tightly and press the button. A series of small blades rotates slowly, mixing the ingredients to a compact and perfectly smooth dough which is ready to be shaped in various ways.

Other mechanical and electric appliances have little plastic or stainless steel discs through which the pasta is drawn to obtain the various shapes.

Nowadays, there is a variety of machines on the market with different features. It is worth investing in one of the more sophisticated machines if you make large quantities of pasta often (the larger machines work best with substantial amounts). Otherwise you may want to experiment at first with the simple and efficient manual pasta machine, or make the pasta entirely by hand as explained below.

To return to homemade pasta, there is basically only one way of making pasta containing exclusively flour and eggs and no other ingredients (see colored pasta on page 26). For homemade pasta the proportions are 1 egg to every 9 to 10 tablespoons of flour, or 6 eggs to every pound (3½ cups), and a little olive oil and water.

Choosing and testing the ingredients - Use all-purpose white flour or hard-wheat flour semolina, which should be very soft to the touch; if you run it through your hands, it should adhere to your fingers and feel slightly oily. Before you start it is a good idea to sift the flour to eliminate any lumps.

The eggs must be very fresh and cold, but not straight out of the refrigerator. They should be kept in a well-ventilated room where the temperature is around 65°F. Excessive heat or excessive cold can have an adverse effect on the basic ingredients and on the texture and elasticity of the dough itself.

There are various methods of testing the freshness of an egg. The fresher an egg is, the smaller the volume of air in the air pocket at its broader end. Immerse the egg in salt water (about ¼ cup salt to 1 quart cold water): a fresh egg will sink to the bottom, not-so-fresh egg will hover above the bottom and eggs which are more than a month old will float on the surface of the water (see the diagram on page 23). To make doubly sure, it is better to break the egg into a bowl before using it: if it is fresh, the yolk will be full and have a convex shape while the white will be very elastic.

Mixing the dough - Heap the flour in a mound and make a hollow in the center. Break the eggs into the hollow and add a little olive oil (if you are using oil) and a few pinches of salt. Begin to work the eggs into the flour, carefully, with your fingertips. When the flour has been completely absorbed by the eggs, knead the dough with both hands for 10 to 15 minutes until the dough is firm, smooth and elastic. While you are kneading the dough, it is a good idea to flour your hands from time to time as you stretch the dough, and fold it back on itself over and over again. Little bubbles will form on the surface indicating

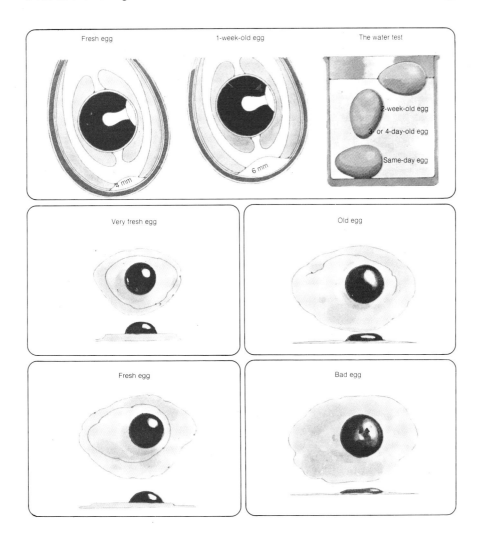

that the dough is sufficiently kneaded. At this point, gather the dough into a ball, dust it with a handful of flour, put it in a lightly floured bowl, cover with a cloth and let it rest for about 15 minutes.

How to stretch the dough by hand - To stretch the dough evenly, first flatten it with the palm of your hand and continue with the help of the rolling pin as follows: flatten the dough by banging it heavily with the rolling pin, working from the center outwards, in all directions, rotating it slowly on the pastry board so that it becomes more or less circular and the same thickness all over. To turn the sheet of dough without breaking it, wrap it round the rolling pin and rotate it gently on the pastry board. When the dough is too unwieldy to be wrapped round completely, repeat the operation but only wrap the top part round the rolling pin, letting the rest fall from the pastry board; the edges will become very thin from the action of the rolling pin while the sheer weight of the sheet of dough will stretch the center. By the end of the process, the sheet of dough should be just a bit more than $1/16$ inch thick.

How to stretch the dough by machine - After mixing and resting the dough, you can speed up the kneading process by using an electric or manual pasta machine. The resulting sheet of dough will not be quite as thin nor have such a fine texture as hand-stretched dough.

The machine kneading process is simple: a piece of dough is passed five or six times through the rollers, set at the maximum distance apart; each time the dough is folded back on itself and a different end is fed into the machine first. Then the distance between the rollers is reduced by turning the appropriate knob and the dough is passed through several times more. The rollers are adjusted until the desired thickness of dough is reached.

How to obtain different shapes - To cut the sheet of dough by hand you will need, as already mentioned, a heavy knife with a very sharp, wide blade.

Leave the sheet of dough on the pastry board to dry for a short while, though not too long or the pasta will dry out.

Tagliatelle or fettucce

To make tagliatelle or fettucce roll up the sheet of dough into a long narrow sausage. Then cut strips $1/8$ inch wide and unroll each coil by hand, separating the noodles on the pastry board to allow them to dry out.

Tagliatelle are generally served with a vegetable sauce or with any kind of *ragù* (meat sauce such as Bolognese sauce).

Fettuccine, linguine, lagane or laganelle
Proceed as for tagliatelle but make the strips about ⅛ inch wide.
Serve with butter and cheese, with cream or with béchamel sauce.

Tagliatelline, tagliolini or taglierini
Proceed as for tagliatelle but cut the strips very fine, about ⅛ inch wide. Try not to squash the roll of dough as you make clean, sharp cuts. Unroll each coil as soon as you have cut it as it will tend to stick together.
Usually served in meat broth, they are also excellent with cheese and butter or with a fresh tomato sauce.

Maltagliati
The dough is rolled up as for tagliatelle and the same sharp wide-bladed knife is used. This time, cut zig-zag strips about ½ inch wide: you will end up with irregular diamond-shaped pieces — hence the name *maltagliati* which means "badly cut".
Maltagliati are usually cooked in vegetable soup, especially with chick peas or beans.

Quadrettini or quadrucci
Roll the dough up in the usual way. Cut strips about ½ inch wide, then turn each rolled-up coil round and cut it across into little pieces about ½ inch long. This will give you little squares that should immediately be separated and left to dry on the pastry board.
Cook in meat or vegetable broth.

Pappardelle or reginette
Leave the dough stretched out in a thin sheet. Using a serrated wooden pastry wheel, cut the dough into long strips ¾ to 1¼ inches wide.
Serve with rich meat sauces (especially those made with game or giblets) or with mushrooms.

Farfalle, nodini or galani

Again starting with the sheet of dough, and before it has become too dry, use the serrated wooden pastry wheel to cut horizontal strips $1/2$ to $3/4$ inch wide (depending on whether you intend to cook the shapes in soup or for a main course). Then, without moving the strips, make vertical cuts $1 1/2$ to 2 inches apart: this will give you rectangles which you pinch in the center to create the distinctive butterfly shape.

Depending on the size of the farfalle, serve with tomato sauce, Bolognese sauce, with the juices from roast meat or stews, or in vegetable soups.

Lasagna noodles

Using either the knife or the wooden pastry wheel, cut strips about 3 to 4 inches wide from the sheet of dough. Cut these strips into rectangles or squares of the required length.

Classically, lasagna is baked in the oven with a very rich Bolognese sauce and a béchamel sauce, or the noodles are rolled up and made into cannelloni which are then stuffed with meat, ricotta and green vegetables, or with cheese and ham.

Pasta grattugiata or pasta tritata

Mix the pasta dough as described but add a little more flour to give it a firmer consistency. After kneading and resting the dough divide it into pieces and roll each piece into a ball. Grate each ball against a metal grater, letting the flakes fall on to the floured pastry board. Allow them to dry thoroughly before cooking. Grated pasta is best cooked in meat or vegetable broths.

COLORED PASTA

Colored pasta is prepared in the same way as plain pasta, with a slight modification of the basic ingredients (flour and eggs) and the addition of other ingredients which not only color the pasta but give it a different flavor.

The dough must be colored only with natural ingredients carefully measured depending on the color you wish to obtain. Certain ingredients, like cocoa, saffron and paprika, should be added to the dough in tiny amounts because their flavor must not become overpowering.

Green pasta, made with spinach

For every pound (3½ cups) flour, allow 8 ounces of fresh spinach, 4 "large" eggs and a pinch of salt. Wash the spinach and boil it without adding any water, only a pinch of salt. Let the spinach cool and squeeze it out by hand before putting it through a vegetable mill. Add the spinach to the flour and eggs and make the dough as described earlier. If the spinach has retained too much moisture you may need to add a little more flour. Then roll out the dough and cut out the required shapes. Green pasta is slightly less elastic than plain pasta and the sheet of dough will not be so transparently thin. It is advisable to divide it into several pieces and roll them out one at a time, covering the others with a cloth to prevent them from drying out.

Green pasta, made with mint

For every pound (3½ cups) flour, allow a large handful of fresh mint, 4 "large" eggs and a pinch of salt.
Boil the mint with a pinch of salt, drain, and dry it thoroughly with paper tissue. Put it through a sieve or food mill. Add the mint to the other ingredients with a little water or milk (about 2 tablespoons) if the eggs are not sufficient to bind the flour. Roll out the dough and cut out tagliatelle about ¼ inch wide. Mint pasta can be served with butter and cheese, or with fresh cream and cheese.

Grey-green pasta, made with nettles

For every pound (3½ cups) flour allow 4 ounces fresh nettles, 4 "large" eggs and a pinch of salt.
Wash the nettles carefully. Boil the leaves with a pinch of salt, drain, and dry well; then put through a sieve or food mill. Add the nettles to the other ingredients with a little water if the eggs are not sufficient to bind the flour. Roll out the dough and cut out tagliatelle about ½ inch wide.

Beige pasta, made with mushrooms
For every pound (3 ½ cups) flour, allow 4 ounces dried cèpes-wood mushrooms, 4 "large" eggs and a pinch of salt.
Soften the mushrooms by soaking them in a little warm water for a few minutes. Drain, keeping the water, and fry the mushrooms gently in oil with a little white wine and stock. Cook until the mushrooms are soft and the liquid has completely evaporated. Put the mushrooms through a sieve or food mill and mix the purée with the other ingredients, adding a few teaspoonfuls of the water the mushrooms had soaked in (strain it first). Add more flour to obtain a fairly firm dough. Roll out the dough as thin as possible and cut into your favorite shape.

Yellow pasta, made with pumpkin
For every pound (3 ½ cups) flour, allow 1 pound pumpkin and 3 "large" eggs.
Cut the pumpkin into slices, peel them and discard the seeds. Bake until tender in the oven (you can also boil the pieces in salted water but the pumpkin will retain more moisture). Put the pumpkin through a food mill. If the purée is too liquid, dry it out gently in a saucepan over low heat, stirring continuously. Add it to the other ingredients and make the dough as described earlier, adding more flour if necessary.

Bright orange pasta, made with carrots
For every pound (3 ½ cups) flour, allow 8 ounces of new sweet carrots and 3 eggs.
Scrape the carrots, trim the ends, and steam or boil them in a little lightly salted water. Drain and put through a food mill. If the purée is too liquid, heat in a saucepan over very low flame. Continue as for yellow pasta.

Red pasta, made with tomatoes
For every pound (3 ½ cups) flour, allow 1 ½ tablespoons tomato paste, 6 "large" eggs, and salt.
Proceed as for plain pasta adding the tomato paste to the eggs before mixing them with the flour. To obtain a brighter color, add more tomato paste.

Purple pasta, made with beets
For every pound (3 ½ cups) flour, allow 1 large cooked beet, 4 "large" eggs and a pinch of salt.
Peel the beet, cut the flesh into small pieces and put through a food mill, letting the purée fall into a dish lined with cheesecloth. Bring the edges of the cheesecloth together and squeeze the excess juice out of the beet. Then add the purée left in the cheesecloth to the flour, eggs and salt and proceed as usual. The amount of flour can be varied depending on how much beet purée is obtained. This pasta is not particularly elastic and cannot be rolled out very thin.
It is advisable, when cutting the sheet of dough, to sprinkle it with a little corn meal or fine semolina to make it easier to roll up. It is best to work quickly because purple pasta soon dries out.

Brown pasta, made with cocoa
For every pound (3 ½ cups) flour, allow ⅓ cup unsweetened cocoa and 6 "large" eggs. You can add less cocoa if you prefer a lighter pasta with a less pronounced flavor.
Follow the same procedure as for plain pasta, adding the sifted cocoa to the flour.
This particular type of pasta should be served with game, pigeon or duck.

Bright yellow pasta, made with saffron
For every pound (3 ½ cups) flour, allow ⅛ to ¼ teaspoon saffron, 6 "large" eggs and a pinch of salt.
Crumble the saffron and dissolve it in very little warm water. Add the solution to the eggs in the center of the mound of flour and proceed as for plain pasta.

White pasta, made with cheese
This type of pasta is called "white" to distinguish it from plain pasta. In fact it has a yellow color because of the eggs, but it is a pale, faded yellow that is very nearly white.
It is very tasty and therefore requires a simple, delicately flavored seasoning, such as fresh melted butter or a tomato sauce.
For every half pound (1 ¾ cups) flour, allow a half pound (2 cups) gra-

ted Parmesan cheese and 4 "large" eggs. Grate the cheese very finely and add it to the flour, then add the eggs and proceed as for plain pasta.

This type of pasta cannot be kept long because of its cheese content.

Blue pasta, made with liqueur

For every pound (3½ cups) flour, allow 3 "large" eggs, a little water and 3 tablespoons blue Curaçao.

Add the water and the liqueur to the flour and eggs and mix to a fairly firm dough. Continue to make the pasta as described before. For a clearer blue color use only the whites of the eggs and add more water. This type of pasta, with its distinctive color and flavor, should be served with a delicately flavored white sauce, butter and cheese, or cream and cheese.

Pink pasta, made with tomatoes and cream

For every pound (3½ cups) flour, allow ¼ cup heavy cream, 1 teaspoon of tomato paste (use the variety sold in tubes), and 5 "large" eggs. Mix the tomato paste with the cream and add to the flour and eggs. Proceed as for plain pasta.

Pink pasta, made with strawberries

For every pound (3½ cups) flour, allow 4 ounces strawberries, 4 "large" eggs, a pinch of salt and a little milk or heavy cream.

Purée the strawberries in a blender or by pressing them through a fine sieve. Add the strawberry purée to the flour, eggs, salt and a little milk or cream. If the dough is too wet, add a handful of flour. Then roll out the dough, which tends to be delicate, twice, into a sheet that is not too thin, and cut thin fettuccine.

You should eat strawberry pasta at once and serve it with a white sauce having a cream and cheese base, or simply with melted butter and Parmesan cheese.

Black pasta, made with squid ink

For every pound (3½ cups) flour allow the ink of 8 squid, 5 "large" eggs and a little water.

Dissolve the squid ink, which is contained in a sac inside the mollusc, in a little cold water and add to the flour and eggs. Add enough water to make a medium-firm dough. Roll out the dough as thin as possible, adding flour if necessary, and cut out the required shapes. This type of pasta is only served with fish sauces made with squid, shellfish, or the like, and without cheese. You can add more flavor by sprinkling with chopped fresh herbs just before serving.

This type of pasta is grey rather than black because the eggs tone down the deep black of the ink.

STUFFED PASTA

Stuffed pasta includes all the different types of pasta which have some kind of filling — whether meat, vegetables, cheese or fish — and which vary in shape and size according to the culinary traditions of the different regions. Stuffed pasta is served on its own, with sauces or in broth.

Meat stuffings are made with beef, veal, pork or turkey, usually ground, cooked or uncooked, and sometimes mixed with ham, mortadella, sausage, or giblets. Meat-based fillings are usually flavored with spices, cheese and eggs, which also help to bind the stuffing.

Then there are fillings made from meat and vegetables, or vegetables and cheese. Among the most commonly used vegetables are spinach, chard, asparagus, lettuce and pumpkin. Breadcrumbs mixed with cheese and sausage makes an economical filling, and there are stuffings containing fish or fish mixed with boiled vegetables.

Depending on their shape, filling and region of origin, the stuffed pastas have different names: agnolini, agnolotti, ravioli, cappelletti, tortellini, calzoncini, ofelle, cannelloni, pasticci, rotoli and crêpes. All these preparations take time to make, which is why it is advisable to prepare the stuffing in advance and to have the appropriate utensils.

As well as the usual pastry board and rolling pin, or machine to save time and effort, you will also find the following useful: a serrated or smooth pastry wheel, a very sharp knife, round and square molds, and, for certain dishes like cannelloni, pasticci, and crêpes, a range of baking dishes.

agnolotti with tomato sauce

Agnolini and agnolotti

Agnolini are a specialty of Mantua in Lombardy and agnolotti come from Piedmont.

Stuffings for agnolini vary from city to city and even from one family to another. Agnolini can be served simply with butter and cheese or with milk and cheese, or they can be cooked in a beef or chicken broth.

To prepare agnolini: mix the dough using the same proportions of flour and eggs as in the basic recipe for plain pasta (page 23). It is a good idea to make the dough a little softer, so add a little water if necessary. Roll out the dough very thin. Try to work in a cool but draft-free room to protect the dough from drying out before it is stuffed and shaped. As soon as the dough has been rolled out, use the pastry wheel to cut the dough into squares each measuring $1\frac{1}{4} \times 1\frac{1}{4}$ inches for the agnolini and $2\frac{1}{2} \times 2\frac{1}{2}$ inches for the agnolotti. Take a small quantity of stuffing and place it in the center of the square, then fold the corners together to make a triangle. Press the edges together so that the dough adheres perfectly (this ensures that the stuffing will not come out during cooking). At the same time, wrap the pasta around your forefinger, overlapping and joining the two opposite corners. While you are doing this, the third corner will fold under by itself.

Agnolini and agnolotti can also be made from round shapes. To make these, cut discs from the sheet of dough and proceed as described above.

Tortellini or cappelletti

These are an Emilian specialty, from Bologna to be precise. Tortellini are nearly always served in broth, but can be accompanied by tomato or Bolognese sauce.

To prepare tortellini: roll out the dough as usual; take small quantities of stuffing and place them $\frac{3}{4}$ to $1\frac{1}{4}$ inches apart in a row about $1\frac{1}{4}$ inches from the edge of the sheet of dough. Then fold over the outer edge of the dough to cover the little mounds of stuffing. Cut off the strip of stuffed pasta with the pastry wheel, and press the dough down around each mound of filling to hold it in. Still using the pastry wheel cut up the strip of stuffed pasta into little rectangles. To finish,

tortellini with cream sauce in vol-au-vent

overlap the two bottom corners of the rectangle to give the tortellini the shape of a little hat.

Ravioli
Ravioli are perhaps the best known type of stuffed pasta. They can be either square or rectangular in shape and are common in many parts of Italy. The name *raviolo* is an ancient word for describing pasta that is *riavvolta* (wrapped around) a filling. Ravioli is served with a variety of sauces: mushroom, tomato, meat and many others.

To prepare ravioli: roll out the dough and place little mounds of stuffing about 1½ inches apart in a row about 1½ inches from the edge of the sheet of dough. Fold the outer edge of the dough over the mounds of stuffing, then cut off the strip of stuffed pasta with the pastry wheel and press the dough down around the filling to seal it tightly. Finally, use the pastry wheel to divide the strip into fairly large rectangles of filled pasta. If you are making ravioli for soup, make smaller ones.

Panciuti or pansoti
These are fat or bulging ravioli, and are a typical pasta from Genoa in Liguria. They are triangular or round in shape and stuffed with a filling of cheese, eggs and herbs. In the classic Ligurian recipe they are served with a sauce made from walnuts, pine nuts and bread diluted with milk and olive oil (see recipe on page 162). They are also good with melted butter and cheese.

Make the dough with flour, water and white wine (using more water than wine) to obtain a medium-firm consistency. Roll out the dough in a thin sheet and cut out triangles with sides 2½ to 3 inches long or discs with a diameter of about 2½ to 3 inches. As you cut out the shapes, keep them covered with a cloth to stop them from drying out. Then fill each triangle or disc with the prepared stuffing and fold the edges over, making sure you seal them tightly.

Calzoncini or casonsei
Calzoncini are a kind of large ravioli, a typical pasta from Brescia in Lombardy, and consist of half-moon shapes filled with bread soaked in milk and mixed with sausage and cheese. They are served with

pumpkin ravioli with ragù

— 36 —

melted butter and Parmesan cheese (see the recipe on page 159).

Make the usual egg pasta dough and roll it out into a thin sheet. Then cut rectangles each measuring about 3×5 inches. Put a mound of stuffing in the center of each rectangle and fold the dough lengthwise. Press the sides down around the stuffing, then, holding the edges of the rectangle with your fingers, pull the edges down to give the ravioli the shape of calzoncini.

Ofelle

These are a square sort of ravioli from the Friuli-Venezia Giulia region and are stuffed with spinach, veal and sausage. They are served with butter and Parmesan cheese (see the recipe on page 161).

To prepare ofelle: mix the flour with some mashed potato, eggs, yeast (to lighten the dough) and salt to obtain a dough rather like that used to make potato gnocchi (dumplings). Then roll out the dough as thin as possible (it is very fragile and you will not be able to roll it out as thin as the plain flour and egg dough). Cut the dough into squares measuring $2\frac{1}{2}$ to 3 inches and put the stuffing on half the squares. Cover with the remaining squares, pressing the pasta down firmly to seal in the filling.

Tortelli con la coda

This variety of stuffed pasta has the distinctive shape of a twisted sweet and is filled with spinach, ricotta, cream cheese, Parmesan cheese and eggs. It is served with melted butter, sage and Parmesan, or with tomato sauce.

To prepare tortelli con la coda: make the plain egg pasta dough and roll out the dough as thin as possible. Place little mounds of filling 3 to 4 inches apart on the sheet of dough. Then fold the dough over the filling to enclose it. Cut off the filled strip in the usual way and press the pasta down around the filling. Divide the strip into long rectangles. Take the two ends of each rectangle and twist them gently. Continue as if wrapping sweets.

Marubini

A round variety of ravioli which is typical of the town of Cremona, in Lombardy, marubini are filled with a stuffing made from ground

panciuti or pansoti with melted butter

beef, veal, pork sausage or brains, with Parmesan cheese, egg and spices. They are cooked in meat stock and served with Parmesan. They can also be served on their own, drained, with the sauce of your choice (see the recipe on page 160).

To prepare marubini: make the usual egg pasta and divide the dough into two equal parts. Roll out into two thin sheets. Place little mounds of filling on one sheet, ¾ to 1¼ inches apart, and cover with the other sheet of dough, pressing the edges tightly together.

After pressing down the dough around each mound of filling, use a serrated or smooth pastry cutter to cut out the marubini. Then lift away the leftover dough which can be cut up into tiny pieces and cooked in a vegetable soup.

Cannelloni

Cannelloni are little rolls of pasta stuffed with meat or with a mixture of green vegetables and ricotta, or with slivers of ham and cheese. They are eaten all over Italy, from the north to the south.

To prepare cannelloni: make the usual egg pasta dough and roll it out into a fairly thin sheet. Cut out large squares or rectangles. Lay the filling on one half of each square and roll the dough into a tube shape over the filling. Cannelloni are cooked in the oven with a béchamel or tomato sauce, Bolognese or other meat ragù or with a velouté sauce.

Pasta piena

This is a sheet of pasta stuffed and cut into small squares and is a specialty of the Romagna region. The stuffing is usually made from beef marrow, ham, Parmesan cheese, breadcrumbs, spices and egg. The traditional recipe, however, has a simpler filling of soft cheese, Parmesan, egg and salt.

The pasta is cooked in good meat stock and accompanied by grated Parmesan cheese (see the recipe on page 164). If you prefer, you can drain off the broth and serve the pasta with the sauce of your choice.

To prepare pasta piena: make egg pasta dough and roll it out as thin as possible. Then cover half the sheet of dough with the stuffing, smoothing it with a long spatula. Fold over the other half of the dough and seal the edges tightly. Press a little with the rolling pin to make the two layers of dough stick together.

cannelloni with mascarpone

Using a pastry wheel, cut strips about ³/₄ inch wide then cut across the strips to make little squares.

Rotolo
This is a type of large cannellone made from egg pasta and generally filled with a mixture of spinach or chard and ricotta.
To prepare rotolo: roll out the dough into a long, wide rectangle and spread the stuffing over the dough. Roll it up on itself keeping the roll nice and tight and closing the ends as if it were a package. Wrap it in cheesecloth, tie it in several places and poach it in a large quantity of simmering salted water.
Cut into slices about ¹/₂ inch thick and serve with the sauce of your choice (see the recipe on page 168). Rotolo makes a substantial and tasty main dish.

SOME TYPICAL REGIONAL VARIETIES OF PASTA

This section deals with some regional varieties of pasta which are prepared in much the same way as home-made egg pasta. Originating in different regions of Italy, these types of pasta have become well known and are now part of the national gastronomic heritage.
The dough is made by hand and the shapes are formed with the help of presses and other basic utensils.
The flours used are hard-wheat, hard-wheat mixed with all-purpose white flour, whole-wheat flour, buckwheat flour, or white flour mixed with bran. For certain types of pasta, breadcrumbs, chestnut flour, vegetables or eggs are added to the flour.

Bigoli
Bigoli are a typically Venetian pasta resembling thick spaghetti. They are made with hard-wheat flour, or with half hard-wheat flour and half all-purpose white flour (white bigoli), or with whole-wheat flour (dark bigoli), mixed with water. Nowadays bigoli are enriched with other ingredients which make the dough softer and tastier. Bi-

goli can be made by mixing $^3/_4$ pound ($2^2/_3$ cups) of either hard-wheat flour or whole-wheat flour with 4 "large" eggs, salt, 2 tablespoons butter and enough milk to make a fairly stiff dough. The dough is put through the *bigolaro*, a manually operated press, and the long spaghetti-like pasta is collected in a wide floured receptacle or basket, first cut into lengths of about 12 inches as it comes out of the machine. Bigoli are served with various sauces, such as duck sauce, onion and anchovy sauce, fresh sardines sautéed in oil and garlic, or chicken giblet sauce.

Trofie

Trofie are a Ligurian specialty. They are like gnocchi (dumplings) with twisted tapering ends, generally made from white flour and bran. The ratio is $^3/_4$ pound ($2^2/_3$ cups) white flour to 1/3 cup bran mixed with enough slightly salty water to make a firm dough. Sometimes chestnut flour is added in tiny amounts to sweeten the gnocchi and blend with the sauce.

To make trofie, cut the dough into pieces, roll each piece on the floured pastry board to obtain a thin stick shape, then cut off pieces about the size of a chick-pea or a little larger. With your right thumb roll each piece on the pastry board to form a twisted dumpling with tapering ends, measuring about $1^1/_4$ inches in all.

To save time, you can make the gnocchi bigger and flatten them on a fork as for potato gnocchi. Trofie are boiled on their own or sometimes with fresh white beans. They are often served with pesto sauce made by crushing fresh basil, garlic, pine nuts, Romano or Parmesan cheese, salt and lots of olive oil with a mortar and pestle, or a variant of the sauce containing other ingredients such as walnuts, paprika, or chili powder.

Garganelli

A specialty from Romagna, these are a kind of fluted macaroni made from a mixture of white flour and grated Parmesan cheese, eggs, nutmeg and salt. For each pound ($3^1/_2$ cups) flour allow 4 tablespoons grated cheese and 6 "large" eggs. You need a special utensil called a *pettine* (comb) which is a wooden block (made of cane), with ridges on the upper surface and a thin stick.

Mix the flour, cheese, eggs, a few pinches of nutmeg and salt into a dough, then, flouring the pastry board from time to time, roll it out. Keep the bulk of the dough covered with a cloth and cut a little of the dough at a time into 1 ½ inch squares. Then wrap one corner of a square of dough around the thin rod, pressing it over the *pettine*. The ridges on the *pettine* give the macaroni a fluted appearance similar to fluted penne. Remove the garganelli from the rod and continue likewise with the other squares of dough. If you do not have the appropriate utensils, you can use a ridged wooden board (the same as for potato gnocchi) and a round pencil. You can also work directly on the pastry board but the garganelli will come out smooth.
Garganelli are usually served with a bacon sauce.

Pizzoccheri

Pizzoccheri come from the mountainous Valtellina area of Lombardy. They are short fat tagliatelle made with buckwheat flour and water, nowadays, in the proportions of 2 cups buckwheat flour to 1 cup white flour, with 2 "large" eggs, salt and a little milk to form a homogeneous, fairly firm dough. The dough is rolled out into a not-too-thin sheet and cut into strips about ½ inch wide. The strips are then cut into segments 2 to 2½ inches long.
The noodles are cooked in water with the varieties of vegetables eaten in the mountains, such as potatoes and Savoy cabbage, and seasoned with layers of melted butter, sage and whole cloves of garlic alternating with slices of Bitto cheese (you can substitute Fontina). Given the substantial accompaniments (vegetables, cheese and butter), the dish becomes a meal in itself. You can buy commercially produced pizzoccheri in the shops, but they taste nothing like the home-made variety.

Corzetti

Corzetti are a type of pasta from Liguria, so called because their shape is similar to that of the *crosazzo,* the ancient silver coin of the seafaring Republic of Genoa. They are made from white flour, eggs, salt and warm water in sufficient quantities to obtain a stiff dough. Sometimes boiled spinach is added.
In Liguria corzetti are made as follows: the dough is rolled out in

garganelli with bacon sauce

a fairly thick sheet and little discs are cut out with the appropriate mould (a *crosetti* iron) which leaves an arabesque pattern impressed on the discs. To form corzetti at home you can break off little pieces of dough about the size of a chick-pea, stretch and pinch the pieces to form a shape like a full figure 8.

Corzetti are served with alternating layers of melted butter and finely chopped sweet marjoram, with a good pinch of freshly ground black pepper, or with a Bolognese or mushroom sauce.

Ceriole or stringozzi

Ceriole are a typical dish from Umbria. They are a type of very long macaroni with holes in the center and made from hard-wheat flour mixed with salted water in sufficient quantities to obtain a fairly consistent dough. A special iron needle with a square section is used, but a large knitting needle may be used instead.

To make ceriole at home: knead the dough energetically for some time, beating it repeatedly on the pastry board. Roll it into a thick sheet and cut into long wide strips. Flour your hands and roll the iron needle across the strips of dough so that they curl around it. Let them dry a little before removing them.

Ceriole are served with a spicy tomato, garlic and oil sauce, or with heated garlic and oil.

Strozzapreti or strangolapreti

Strozzapreti are a typical dish from Lucca in Tuscany. They are a thin type of crude bucatini, about 2½ inches long and made from white flour and boiling water. Mix the flour and water with a wooden spoon until a dough of the right consistency is obtained — neither too hard nor too soft. To obtain a richer dough add eggs and use less hot water. Then knead the dough by hand on the pastry board for about 15 minutes and shape it into long sticks about the thickness of your little finger. Cut into pieces about 1 inch long. Roll the pieces around a knitting needle to obtain short *bucatini* with a hole in the center. Let dry.

Strozzapreti are served with a meat sauce, Romano cheese and black pepper.

Maccheroni inferrettati or maccaruni

Maccheroni inferrettati are very common all over southern Italy, as well as in Sicily and Sardinia. As the name denotes, these are a type of long macaroni with a hole in the center. They are sometimes called *fusilli*. They are made with white flour and hard-wheat flour mixed with water and salt.

Mix 10 ounces (2 cups) white flour and 5 ounces (1 cup) hard-wheat flour, with sufficient slightly salted water to make a firm dough. Use the appropriate square-sectioned iron needle, or a large knitting needle, or even a stick of willow, which is more supple and easier to manage. Cut the dough into pieces and cover with a cloth to prevent it from drying. Then roll a piece of dough into a cylindrical shape about as thick as a pencil, and cut into lengths of between 2½ to 8 inches depending on how long you want the macaroni to be. Lay 2 or 3 pieces close to each other on the pastry board. Put the needle up against the center of the rolls of dough. Pressing on the needle and on the dough, push the needle into the dough, moving it backwards and forwards to hollow out the center. Remove the macaroni from the needle and allow them to dry on the pastry board. The macaroni can be served in a variety of ways: with tomato and oregano sauce, with tomato, olive and caper sauce, with garlic, oil and sweet peppers or with tomato and eggplant sauce.

Orecchiette

This is a typical pasta from Apulia in southern Italy. It is also known as *strascicati* or *strascinati* (dragged pasta) because it is made by pressing or dragging the dough on a rough wooden table. Orecchiette are shaped like tiny "ears" (hence their name in Italian), shells or hats, and are made from hard-wheat flour and white flour mixed with water and salt. For 3 cups all-purpose flour, allow 1 cup hard-wheat flour and enough warm water to make a fairly firm dough, a little stiffer than that used to make bread.

Break off a piece of dough and roll it on the floured pastry board until it is cylindrical and about the thickness of a pencil. Then cut it into ½ inch lengths. Using a rounded knife like a palette knife, press each piece over the pastry board. The dough will roll up into a shell shape. You can also shape them with the tip of your thumb.

Cook with potatoes or broccoli and season with tomato sauce and cheese. Orecchiette are also made commercially with whole-grain hard-wheat flour.

Malloreddus

A Sardinian specialty, malloreddus are a type of tiny, fluted *gnocchi* (dumplings) made from hard-wheat flour, water and salt. A pinch of saffron may also be added. The shapes are made with an instrument called a *ciurili*, a kind of sieve woven of very fine rush threads or twisted string.

Make a firm (but not too hard) smooth dough, break off a small piece and roll it with your hands to obtain a longish roll about ¼ inch wide. Then break off little peices about the size of a bean and rub them on the rush threads to obtain the distinctive texture and sea-shell shape.

Before cooking, allow to dry for 24 hours. Serve with a sauce made from lamb or game, tomatoes and bacon.

Malloreddus are made commercially from hard-wheat flour.

THE MEDITERRANEAN DIET

Proponents of the "Mediterranean diet" suggest it is the healthiest and most balanced diet there is.

Based on pasta as a staple, it is a diet that isn't a diet, a way of eating healthily, spending less and protecting your health by going back to what was once considered the food of the poor: cereals, vegetables and olive oil.

It is a diet that is advocated by the Italian National Institute of Nutrition, by the health-conscious and by many Italian nutritionists who have endorsed it from the dietary point of view.

It is a diet which is particularly recommended for the prevention and alleviation of cardiovascular disease because it is low in animal fat, meat and sugar.

Let us return therefore to our ancient dishes, to the well-loved home-cooked pasta and to the tasty vegetable soups to make ourselves feel better and healthier.

The father of the Mediterranean diet is Ancel Keys, a world expert on nutrition. Professor Keys has reached the conclusion, based on epidemiological studies made in southern Italy and Greece, that the population in these zones suffer fewer incidents of illness related to over-rich foods and modern-day living.

What do people in the Mediterranean eat? In general they have kept to a post-war tradition of eating food that is usually associated with poverty, such as pasta and legumes, very little meat, and a great deal of fruits and vegetables, with olive oil as a condiment.

Keys is not the only one to reach this conclusion. A special Senate Committee on Nutrition recently came to the same conclusion. The Committee did research to find the ideal diet for combating diabetes, obesity and arteriosclerosis commonly found in industrialized countries.

Based on their studies, they recommend a diet made up of the following components: 55-65% carbohydrates, 12% protein, and 30% fats, of which 65% come from vegetable fats. As a dietary goal, this ideal balance was compared to the actual eating habits of five industrialized countries, among them Italy, and the results showed it to be the same as in Italy during the fifties.

Let us clarify the concept of "diet", a word frequently used to indicate a nutritional plan tied to a specific health problem or more often, to losing weight. In fact, "diet", which comes from the Greek, means life style, especially as it relates to health and food. Thus, following a "Mediterranean diet" does not mean going on a diet, but simply eating certain foods, as natural and fresh as possible, following the eating habits typical of the Mediterranean.

But it is not sufficient simply to eat pasta more often; it is necessary to choose the correct combinations of foods, to select food according to their nutritional content and to individual needs, to serve less sauce and, above all, to make qualitative as well as quantitative choices. It is precisely along these lines that the recipes for pasta dishes in this book have been created and balanced according to the new recommendations of nutritionists.

ADVICE FROM
THE EXPERTS

WHAT MAKES GOOD PASTA?

It is almost impossible to recognize good pasta at first sight, particularly commercially made dried pasta, as it is sold in packages or sealed cellophane bags. One indication of quality is the color which should be even all over. The pasta should have a pleasant smell and should be brittle.

If you break off a piece, you can tell whether or not it has been made from durum wheat because there will be tiny black flecks in the dough. A mixture of hard and soft-wheat will make a pasta of smoother and finer consistency.

The real proof, however, lies in its resistance to cooking. Pasta which has been cooked for the right length of time but which adheres to the pot when drained, looks sticky, disintegrates, or is mushy to eat, is definitely unpleasant. It means that the pasta is of poor quality, made with soft-wheat flour or with old hard-wheat flour, lacking in gluten. It is the gluten which is actually the strong point of pasta: if there is a high percentage of gluten, the pasta will not go soggy when cooked, but if there is a low percentage the starch is released, making the pasta sticky.

When it has been cooked, good pasta should not break or unravel. The water should only be slightly cloudy with excess starch and the pasta should have doubled in volume.

When buying dried pasta, it is best to choose well known brands and, once you have found a good brand that survives the cooking test, stick to it.

As for store-bought fresh pasta, it is important to know that this type of pasta, which enjoys a certain popularity because it is similar to homemade pasta, costs more than dried pasta but has less nutritional worth because it contains such a high proportion of water. Its freshness, then, does not always represent an advantage over dried pasta and you pay dearly for it.

THE TEN GOLDEN RULES

1. Use a large deep pot so the pasta has plenty of room.

2. Use 1 quart of water for every 4 ounces of pasta. It is best to use fairly hard water. The saucepan should be about three-quarters full.

3. Use about 1 tablespoon of salt to each quart of water. It is preferable to use sea salt (which is now available in supermarkets), especially when cooking for people who suffer from hypertension or cardiovascular diseases.

4. Add the salt only when the water has reached the boil and wait until all the salt has dissolved and the water has returned to a boil before putting in the pasta.

5. Add the pasta, whether fresh or dried, all at once and stir immediately with a long cooking fork or wooden spoon. For long varieties of pasta, stir frequently during the cooking to prevent the pasta from sticking together. For short varieties, stir occasionally during the cooking. As you stir, lift the pasta away from the bottom of the pot.

6. To prevent certain long or thin types of pasta (such as tagliatelle, pappardelle, spaghetti and trenette) from sticking together, add a drop of oil to the water.

7. Cook in an uncovered pot over a high heat.

8. For commercially made pasta, follow the instructions on the package concerning cooking time; you could keep a note of any variations you make to suit your own taste. For homemade pasta, follow the instructions given in the recipe. But whatever cooking

time is specified, it is always advisable to taste the pasta to see if it is *al dente* before draining it.

9 Drain the pasta when it is *al dente*, that is, still a little firm. According to nutritionists, pasta is easier to digest when it is not overcooked. As soon as the pasta is done, pour a ladleful of cold water into the saucepan to stop the cooking process at once, then drain.

10 For certain types of pasta that should be precooked and then finished off in the oven (cannelloni and lasagna noodles, for example), make sure the pasta is even more *al dente* than usual when you precook it, and preheat the oven thoroughly so the pasta does not overcook in the second phase either.

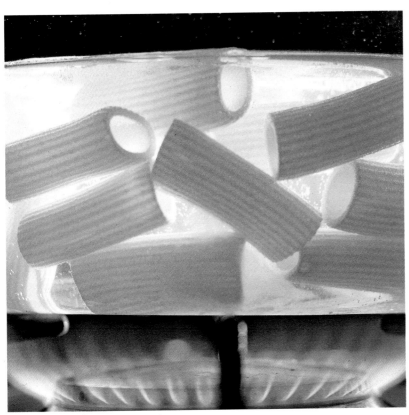

HINTS ON SERVING PASTA

1. Unless you are serving the pasta cold, always warm the bowl or serving dish, either in the oven or by pouring boiling water into it and drying thoroughly.

2. Immediately after draining the pasta and before mixing it with the sauce, add a spoonful of oil or a tablespoon of butter to prevent it from sticking together.

3. Mix the pasta with some of the sauce and serve the rest very hot in a sauceboat (otherwise it will flow to the bottom of the serving dish).

4. When serving cheese with the pasta, add the cheese last of all, or serve it separately, when the pasta has completely absorbed the sauce.

5. Do not serve cheese with fish sauces except when specified in certain regional pasta dishes.

6. Grate the cheese just before serving to retain all its flavor and aroma.

7. Keep jars of fresh and dried herbs, tubes of anchovy and olive paste and the pepper mill within reach; they will be useful for whipping up tasty, first-course pasta dishes.

8. If you want to serve pasta that is a brighter yellow, add a pinch of saffron to the cooking water when it begins to boil.

9. Reserve a little of the water the pasta was cooked in if you are serving it with a sauce made with milk, cream or melted cheese. It will make the sauce softer and smoother.

10. Leftover boiled pasta can be added to soups and reheated briefly. If you have a large quantity of leftover pasta you can freeze it.

SAUCES FOR DIFFERENT TYPES OF PASTA

There are many, many different sauces to accompany both home-made and commercially produced pasta. Each of these sauces is capable of transforming pasta into a tasty and substantial main course. There are cooked and uncooked sauces; those made with or without tomatoes; with or without meat; sauces based on cheese, herbs and spices; vegetable sauces; fish sauces; and delicate white sauces — all obtained from a skillful blending of colors and flavors. To help you in the correct choice of sauce (and it is ultimately a matter of individual taste or preference) here are some suggestions.

For tagliatelle, fettuccine, lagane, laganelle, lasagnette, linguine, trenette, spaghetti (or any other long type of pasta):
— Hot or cold sauces based on fresh or canned tomatoes, vegetables and herbs.
— Quick-to-prepare, piquant sauces made with olive oil, garlic, chili pepper, anchovies.
— Fish sauces, mainly shellfish-based.
— White sauces made from cream, mascarpone (that is, cream cheese) or soft cheeses that melt easily, and often containing curry powder, saffron, nutmeg or other spices.

For fusilli, zite, zitoni, torciglioni, viti, bucatini (or other types of dried twisted or hollow pasta)
— Vegetable sauces based on green vegetables cooked in fresh or canned tomato sauce, and such vegetables as sweet bell peppers, eggplant, zucchini, olives and capers.

For fine spaghetti, capelli d'angelo, egg tagliatelle, vermicelli (or any type of very thin long pasta):
— Dots of butter and grated cheese.
— Melted butter with sage and cheese.
— Sauces made with egg.
— Raw fresh tomato sauces.

For pappardelle, and homemade or commercial tagliatelle:
— "Hunter's style" sauces made with duck, rabbit, pheasant or quail.
— Delicate sauces made with cream, ham and peas.

For macaroni, smooth or ridged penne, mezze maniche, sedani, lumaconi, conchiglioni, pipe, ditaloni, etc. (or any type of short, round tubes):
— Ragù made with ground beef or pork.
— Ragù containing sausage.
— Ragù containing mushrooms.
— Ragù containing giblets.
— Vegetable sauces, especially mushroom and artichoke.
— Stews.

For commercially produced or homemade farfalle and short lasagnette (or any type of small wide strips of pasta):
— Delicate creamy sauces based on cream and cheese, cream and salmon, cream and caviar.
— Sauces based on ricotta and spinach or ricotta and asparagus.
— Butter and puréed zucchini with nutmeg and grated Parmesan cheese.

For short ditalini, little penne, gobbetti, sedanini, avemarie (or other very short varieties of pasta):
— Vegetable sauces, always with a tomato base, particularly those containing dried peas or beans, lentils or chick-peas.

For lasagna noodles, both homemade and commercially produced:
— Ragù made with ground beef or pork.
— Ragù containing sausage.
— Ragù containing mushrooms.
— Fresh or dried mushroom sauces.
— Ragù or tomato sauces that have been enriched with béchamel sauce.

For regional and fresh pasta:
Each type requires a particular sauce, depending on local tradition.

CAN PASTA BE FROZEN?

It most certainly can, provided you follow certain tips to ensure that the pasta is frozen perfectly and will taste like a dish of freshly made pasta.

You can freeze both cooked and uncooked pasta. But what are the advantages? They are numerous. In the first place, it saves time and energy. To make a batch of tagliatelle, for example, that will serve eight people rather than four takes only a tiny bit longer. So, next time you are making a quantity for four, double the ingredients and you will be able to freeze half the pasta to use in emergencies when guests turn up unexpectedly.

How to freeze fresh uncooked pasta - After cutting the dough into the various shapes, let them dry for a while by spreading them out on the pastry board. Then divide (or weigh) the shapes into individual portions and package them for freezing. You can use either plastic bags or well sealed plastic containers. The pasta will keep for several months, depending on the temperature of your freezer or refrigerator freezing compartment. When you use the pasta, cook it immediately without thawing.

You can also freeze filled varieties of uncooked pasta, such as ravioli, tortellini, agnolini and others, for several months. Before freezing filled pasta, spread the pieces on a tray and put them in the freezer for about an hour. This will harden the pieces and prevent them from sticking together once they are inside the freezer bag. Put the pieces in airtight plastic bags, dividing the pasta into portions to suit so that you always thaw only the amount needed. Then label each bag with a self-adhesive label stating the contents, the date of freezing and the maximum length of time it can be frozen.

When you want to use frozen filled pasta, do not thaw it first but put it straight into boiling water or stock, depending on whether you intend to eat it drained with a sauce or in a soup.

How to freeze cooked pasta - The best type of pasta to freeze cooked is the dried, commercially produced pasta made from hard-wheat flour, because it 'resists' cooking better and does not break. It is advisable to choose the larger varieties which do not overcook and stand up better to being reheated in the oven.

Also with egg pasta, the best types for freezing (with a few exceptions) are the dried commercially produced ones rather than home-made pasta, because they stand up to cooking better. To freeze cooked pasta, it is important to follow certain essential rules:

— Use best quality olive oil to season the pasta and in small a-mounts, as the oil content tends to reduce the length of time the pasta can be preserved. It is always possible to add oil once the pasta has been thawed.
— Use salt sparingly when boiling the pasta to begin with and when preparing the sauce: salt tends to dehydrate food.
— Add spices and herbs in small amounts because their flavor may intensify with freezing and subsequent reheating. You can always add more later.
— It is advisable to avoid using cream and egg yolk in the accompanying sauce: they can be added at the last minute.
— You can use frozen raw vegetables in the preparation of vegetable sauces. They can be refrozen after being cooked.
— Be sure that all frozen dishes have a label indicating the content, number of portions, date of cooking, and the expiration date.
— Keep the containers that have been in the freezer longest in front, so as not to keep them in the freezer longer than they should.

And here is what you do:

For plain pasta: the pasta should be cooked *al dente* and drained. Freeze in plastic bags or plastic containers (as with fresh pasta). It is sometimes useful to freeze leftover plain pasta or to cook it and freeze it in preparation for a large party but, on the whole, plain pasta takes little time to cook and will have a better consistency if it is not cooked twice.

For sauced dishes like spaghetti with Bolognese sauce: the pasta should be cooked *al dente* or even slightly firmer than usual. Arrest the cooking by adding a little cold water to the pot, drain the pasta and add the prepared sauce. Allow to cool by placing the dish in a large bowl of cold water (making sure that the water level is not higher than that of the dish). Then pour the pasta into the container to go

in the freezer — use a plastic, glass, earthenware or pyrex container. Bolognese sauce can also be frozen separately.

For filled cannelloni: you can use either homemade or commercial pasta. After cooking the pasta *al dente*, drain, leave to dry and fill with the prepared stuffing. Roll up the cannelloni and lay them in the containers, alternating the sauce and the cheese. If you are using earthenware dishes or containers without lids, cover with plastic wrap or aluminum foil, making the container as airtight as possible. Finally, label the containers with the contents and dates as suggested above and place in the freezer. If you use foil containers (or heat-proof dishes), you can remove the lids and put the containers directly into the oven when you want to reheat the cannelloni.

For lasagna: proceed as for cannelloni.

For rotoli with non-meat fillings: after rolling out the homemade egg pasta into a rectangle (as explained in the recipe on page 168), put in the filling, then roll it up in a sausage shape and wrap it in cheese-cloth to bind it. Put the roll in a plastic bag and freeze. Remove from the freezer several hours in advance and allow to thaw partially, then immerse the roll (still wrapped in the cloth) in a large pot of lightly salted boiling water, and boil for 40 minutes to 1 hour (depending on how much the roll has thawed) over moderate heat to prevent the roll from breaking. Slice while it is hot, and serve with melted butter, sage and Parmesan cheese, or with a cream and mushroom sauce.

How long can pasta dishes be kept in the freezer? - This depends on the ingredients: the heavier the sauce and the more oil it contains, the shorter the time it will keep. As a guideline, a pasta dish can be kept in the freezer for up to three months. After that it will gradually begin to lose some of its quality, texture, flavor and aroma. This recommendation is for a freezer at a temperature of between −13° to −22°F. Pasta can be kept for up to six months at a lower temperature still.

How to thaw and reheat pasta - There are several methods: some are appropriate for plain pasta and others for sauced pasta dishes or for dishes that are cooked in the oven with fillings. Plain pasta should be thawed in the refrigerator until it comes free from the sides of the container. Then plunge it into boiling water. When the water returns to a boil the pasta is heated through. Sauced pasta dishes, such as spaghetti with Bolognese sauce, are thawed by keeping the sealed container at room temperature for a few hours. The pasta is then transferred to a *bain-marie* or double boiler and heated over simmering water. When the pasta is sufficiently hot, you can add the final seasonings of herbs, cheese, salt and pepper.

Alternatively, as soon as you take the container out of the freezer, you can immerse it in a pan half filled with boiling water off the heat; when the pasta has come free from the sides of the container, transfer it to a *bain-marie* or double boiler to reheat it.

A third method (if you have time) is to take the container out of the freezer and place it in the bottom of the refrigerator for twenty-four hours. The following day, transfer the contents to a *bain-marie* or double boiler and reheat gently.

Lasagna and other types of filled pasta should be thawed in the bottom of the refrigerator or at room temperature, then remove the lid and place on the center of the oven at 350-400°F. After about a quarter of an hour, cover the top with aluminum foil to stop the surface from burning before the lasagna is heated all the way through. Remove the aluminum foil 5 minutes before serving. Add a few tablespoons of butter or a few spoonfuls of cream and a little cheese if desired.

You can also put lasagna (and any other type of filled pasta) straight from the freezer into the oven. If you do this, keep the oven low at 300°F for at least 30 minutes to thaw the pasta (you can test if it is thawed by plunging a fork into the center). Turn the oven up to 400°F to heat the dish through and obtain a golden-brown top.

If you have a microwave oven the whole process is much simpler and faster: as soon as you take the container out of the freezer, put it in the microwave; within a few minutes it is ready to be served at the table. Follow the manufacturer's instruction book for settings and time, including 'standing time' for thawing.

PASTA WITH RAGÙ
(MEAT SAUCES)

A ragù is a meat sauce made in the same way as a meat stew. Bolognese sauce is the best-known example but there are many variations. Ragù can be made from ground beef, veal or pork, giblets or a combination of various red and white meats, which are simmered gently with a mixture of sautéed chopped vegetables (onions, carrots, celery, garlic), flavored with aromatic herbs (parsley, basil, sage, rosemary, bay leaves) and moistened with either stock or wine. At one time, especially in central and southern Italy, ragù was made, not from ground meat, but from a large piece of beef that was cooked very slowly until it disintegrated and blended in with the sauce. Nowadays, ground meat is used to save time and money.

The recommended cuts of meat are economical rather than prime cuts or those that are part lean and part fat, like blade and shoulder, brisket and thin rib of beef. Sometimes sausage, ham or bacon is used alone or added to ground meat to improve the flavor and texture of the ragù. There are two types of ragù: "red" ragù, which is made with tomatoes, and "white" ragù, which does not include tomatoes. There are also many regional variations. Tasty, piquant sauces are made from game cooked with a mixture of chopped vegetables and ham, or lamb and kid with herbs and spices. The meats are simmered slowly while, during cooking, various liquids are added depending on the local tradition (dry white wine, red wine, liqueur-like wines such as Marsala, Madeira or Vin Santo), or the sauce may be completed by adding some good (preferably homemade) stock.

The recipes that follow will serve 6 as a first course or 4 as a main course.

Fusilli with sausage and mushroom ragù

Time: 45 minutes
Ingredients:
1 lb fusilli
10 oz mushrooms
3 tbsp olive oil
2 tbsp butter
1 onion, finely chopped
1 carrot, finely chopped
1 bay leaf
8 oz spicy Italian sausage
1 lb canned peeled tomatoes
salt and pepper
a few tbsp stock

Wipe the mushrooms with a damp cloth and slice them. Heat the oil and butter in a large pan and sauté the onion and carrot gently. Add the bay leaf, the sliced sausage and the sliced mushrooms. Sauté gently. Force the tomatoes through a fine sieve and add them to the other ingredients in the pan. Add salt and pepper to taste and a few spoonfuls of stock; cover the pan and simmer over a low heat until the sauce thickens. Before removing the pan from the heat, stir in the mixed herbs.
Put the fusilli in a pot of boiling salted water, and cook until the pasta is *al dente*. Drain the pasta and serve with the hot ragù.

Hint: It is preferable to use fresh herbs when available as they have a lot more flavor. Always add them at the last minute.

Spaghetti with bacon

Time: 30 minutes
Ingredients:
1 lb spaghetti or bucatini
4 oz bacon or smoked ham
4 to 5 tbsp olive oil
1 small onion, finely chopped
1 small chili pepper
8 oz peeled tomatoes
salt
2 oz (¹/₂ cup) grated Romano cheese

Cut the bacon or ham into small pieces. Heat the oil in a large pan and sauté the bacon until cooked. Remove from the pan, drain and set aside. Sauté the onion and chili pepper in the same oil.
Cut the tomatoes into fine strips and add to the pan.
Add salt and simmer for a few minutes. Complete the sauce by adding the sautéed bacon and simmering for a few more minutes.
Meanwhile, cook the spaghetti in a large pot of boiling, salted water. Drain the pasta when it is

spaghetti with bacon

al dente and serve with the sauce and grated cheese.

Hint: The best cheese to use is a pungent mature Romano, but if not available, use grated Parmesan.

Maltagliati with ragù

Time: 1½ hours
Ingredients:
1 lb maltagliati
  (diamond-shaped pasta)
4 tbsp butter
2 tbsp olive oil
1 small onion, finely chopped
4 oz ground beef or pork
a few fresh basil leaves
salt
1 lb ripe tomatoes, peeled
  seeded and chopped
2 oz (½ cup) grated Parmesan
  cheese

Prepare the ragù first: heat the butter and the oil in a medium-sized pan and sauté the finely chopped onion until soft. Add 2 tbsp of water.

After 5 minutes, add the ground meat and let it absorb the flavors for a few minutes. Add the basil leaves and tomatoes. Add salt to taste and cook the ragù for about 1 hour over a moderate heat, stirring from time to time.

Preheat the oven to 350°F. Cook the maltagliati in a large pot of boiling, salted water and drain well. Arrange the pasta in layers in a baking dish, spooning a little ragù between each layer. The last layer should be of ragù. Put the dish in the oven for 15 minutes, which is just long enough to brown the top of the pasta. Serve with the grated cheese.

Hint: To make the ragù even tastier, use half ground beef and half ground pork or sausage.

Penne with pork ragù

Time: 1 hour
Ingredients:
1 lb penne
3 to 4 tbsp olive oil
2 oz bacon, diced
1 onion, chopped
1 carrot, chopped
1 tbsp chopped basil and parsley
8 oz ground pork
salt and pepper
½ cup red wine
10 oz canned peeled tomatoes
a few tbsp stock (optional)

Heat 3 to 4 tbsp of oil in a pan and sauté the diced bacon, then add the chopped onion, carrot and herbs. Leave to cook for a minute or two. Add the ground pork, salt and pepper and, when the meat is browned, pour in the red wine. Simmer until the wine has evaporated, force the tomatoes through a fine sieve and add to the other ingredients. Cover and cook the ragù over a low heat, stirring occasionally. Add a little boiling water from time to time or, better still, water and a little stock.

Boil the penne in salted water, drain the pasta when it is *al dente* and serve with the ragù.

Hint: Fresh tomatoes may be substituted for the canned peeled tomatoes.

Macaroni with meatball ragù

Time: 1 hour
Ingredients:
1 lb small ribbed macaroni
1 slice bread, crust discarded
2 tbsp milk
10 oz ground beef
4 oz cooked ham or mortadella,
  chopped
1 tbsp chopped parsley mixed
  with 1 crushed clove garlic
2 oz (½ cup) grated Parmesan
  cheese
a pinch of grated nutmeg
1 egg
salt

1 small onion, chopped
3 to 4 tbsp oil
a small bunch of fresh basil
14 oz canned peeled tomatoes or
¾ cup homemade tomato sauce

Soften the bread in the milk, then squeeze out the excess milk. Mix the ground beef, the chopped ham, parsley, cheese, nutmeg, egg, bread and salt in a bowl. Make little balls of the mixture, about the size of cherries.

Sauté the onion in three or four tablespoons of hot oil in a saucepan.

Add the bunch of basil and the tomatoes. Salt, and simmer until the sauce has reduced. Remove the basil and add the meatballs. Simmer for about 15 minutes, stirring occasionally.

Boil the pasta in a large pot of salted water, drain when it is *al dente* and pour part of the sauce over the macaroni. Transfer the pasta to the middle of a round, fairly deep dish, arrange the meatballs around the outside with a little sauce and serve with the rest of the sauce in a sauceboat.

Hint: Serve as a main course, as the meatball sauce makes a fairly substantial meal. As an accompaniment you could serve a mixed raw vegetable salad, depending on the season.

Conchiglie with frankfurters

Time: 40 minutes
Ingredients:
1 lb conchiglie
4 tbsp olive oil
1 small onion, chopped
1 slice smoked bacon, diced
8 oz frankfurters
10 oz canned peeled tomatoes
(or ½ cup tomato purée)
salt and pepper
a bunch of fresh basil

Heat the oil, and sauté the onion, then add the bacon to the onion. Dip the frankfurters in boiling water for a few seconds, remove the skin, slice and add to the browned onions and bacon. Force the tomatoes through a fine sieve, and add to the other ingredients, stirring well. Add salt and pepper, and the basil leaves. Simmer, stirring from time to time until the ragù has thickened.
Cook the conchiglie in boiling salted water, drain when the pasta is *al dente* and serve with the ragù.
Hint: Serve with grated Parmesan cheese if you wish.

Torciglioni with sausages

Time: 30 minutes
Ingredients:
1 lb torciglioni
(dried pasta twists)
10 oz canned peeled tomatoes
(or ½ cup tomato purée)
1 onion, finely chopped
a few fresh or dried sage leaves
salt and pepper
⅓ cup stock
2 tbsp olive oil
10 oz Italian sausages

Force the tomatoes through a fine sieve into a saucepan and add the onion, the sage leaves, salt pepper, and a little stock. Simmer. Meanwhile, heat the oil in a frying pan and sauté the sausages for about 15 minutes. Drain off the fat and add the sausages to the tomato sauce which will have reduced and thickened. Simmer for another 15 minutes, adding more stock if necessary.
Boil the torciglioni in a large pot of salted water, drain when the pasta is *al dente*, and place on a serving dish.
Pour some of the sauce over the pasta and arrange the sausages around the dish. Then pour over the rest of the simmering sauce.

torciglioni with sausages

Hint: A food mill can always be used in place of a sieve for puréeing tomatoes.

Garganelli with bacon sauce

Time: 1 ½ hours
Ingredients:
1 lb garganelli or fusilli
salt and pepper
3 to 4 tbsp olive oil
5 oz smoked bacon, diced
¾ cup tomato sauce

Spread the garganelli out on a pastry board and when they are dry, cook them in a large pot of boiling salted water. Heat the olive oil in a large frying pan and sauté the bacon.
Drain the pasta when it is *al dente* and add to the smoked bacon.
Then add the well-seasoned tomato sauce, mix well and remove the pan from the heat. Before serving, sprinkle liberally with freshly ground pepper.
Hint: If you do not have the appropriate utensil for making the pasta squares, roll them around a stick on the pastry board. If you wish, you may complete the seasoning with grated Romano cheese.

Orecchiette with veal and pork rolls

Time: 1 ¾ hours
Ingredients:
1 lb fresh or dried orecchiette
10 oz very thin veal scaloppine
10 oz thinly sliced pork loin
salt and pepper
5 oz smoked bacon, chopped
5 oz (1 ¼ cups) grated Parmesan
  and Romano cheeses
a bunch of fresh parsley,
  chopped
2 to 3 tbsp olive oil
1 small onion, chopped
½ cup full-bodied red wine
8 oz canned peeled tomatoes
  (or ½ cup tomato purée)

Spread the slices of veal and pork on the kitchen table, sprinkle with salt and a pinch of pepper and scatter some of the chopped bacon, grated cheese and parsley on top. Roll up the meat into roulades, taking care to keep the stuffing in, and fasten the ends with toothpicks. Heat 2 to 3 tbsp of oil in a large pan and sauté the onion. Add the meat roulades and brown all over. Pour in the red wine and allow to evaporate completely. Force the tomatoes through a fine sieve and add them to

orecchiette with Italian-style meat ragù (p. 74)

the other ingredients in the pan. Simmer until the sauce thickens. A few minutes before removing from the heat, add a handful of cheese.

Boil the orecchiette in a large pot of lightly salted water, drain when the pasta is *al dente* and place on a serving dish. Pour some of the sauce and the rest of the cheese over the pasta and arrange the little rolls around the edge with the rest of the sauce. Serve at once.

Hint: Orecchiette can also be served "in bianco", that is, in a sauce made from best-quality extra-virgin olive oil, garlic, mashed anchovy fillets and boiled turnip tops.

Orecchiette with Italian-style meat ragù

Time: 1 ½ hours
Ingredients:
1 lb fresh or dried orecchiette
⅓ oz dried mushrooms
1 ½ tbsp butter
2 to 3 tbsp olive oil
1 oz smoked ham, sliced
1 oz bacon, sliced
1 carrot, sliced
1 onion, sliced
1 stalk celery, chopped
1 clove garlic, sliced
1 clove
8 oz ground beef
4 oz ground veal
salt and pepper
1 bouquet garni of fresh thyme, marjoram and a bay leaf (optional)
3 tbsp red wine
1 tbsp flour
8 oz peeled tomatoes
2 oz (½ cup) grated Romano cheese

Soak the mushrooms in warm water, drain and slice them. Heat the butter and oil in a large pan and sauté the sliced mushrooms, ham, bacon, carrot, onion, celery and garlic for a few minutes. Add the clove, the ground beef and veal, and salt and pepper to taste. Stir. As soon as the meat begins to brown, add the bouquet garni, and pour in the wine. Cook for 30 minutes. When the sauce has reduced, thicken it, adding the flour.

Force the tomatoes through a fine sieve and add them to the pan. Simmer for another 30 minutes.

Boil the orecchiette in salted water, drain and serve with the hot ragù and grated Romano cheese.

Hint: Even without the fresh

herbs, which are not always available, the ragù will still be tasty. If you like, you can add more dried mushrooms, which are available in packets from specialty food shops.

Fettuccine with Bolognese sauce

Time: 1½ hours
Ingredients:
1 lb fresh or dried fettuccine
1 oz dried mushrooms
1 tbsp butter
1 small onion, chopped
½ carrot, chopped
1 stalk celery, chopped
a bunch of fresh parsley,
  chopped
1 clove garlic (optional)
1 oz bacon, chopped
8 oz ground pork
1 tbsp dry white wine
3 tbsp tomato paste
salt and pepper
a pinch of sugar (optional)
a pinch of nutmeg
2 chicken livers, chopped
2 oz (½ cup) grated Parmesan
  cheese

Soak the mushrooms in warm water. Heat the butter in a large pan and sauté the chopped onion, carrot, celery, parsley, garlic and bacon for about 10 minutes. Then add the ground meat and brown it. Pour in the wine and, after a few minutes, add the tomato paste mixed with a little warm water. Add salt, pepper, sugar, nutmeg, the drained, coarsely chopped mushrooms and the chicken livers. Add the water drained from the mushrooms to the sauce, filtering it first. Cover the pan and cook over a low heat for about 1 hour, stirring from time to time. Cook the fettuccine in a large pot of boiling salted water and drain when the pasta is *al dente*. Serve with the hot ragù and grated cheese.

Hint: If you wish, you may add a few tablespoonfuls of heavy cream to the ragù. You can also use 10 ounces of fresh tomatoes instead of tomato paste.

Fettuccine with basil-flavored sauce

Time: 1 hour 40 minutes
Ingredients:
1 lb fresh or dried fettuccine
1 tbsp butter
1 tbsp olive oil
1 very small onion, chopped
2 lb very small ripe tomatoes,
  peeled

— 75 —

salt and freshly ground pepper
a large bunch of fresh basil

Heat the butter and oil in a pan and brown the chopped onions. Press the tomatoes through a sieve and add to the onion, together with salt and pepper. Simmer for half an hour, stirring from time to time.

Boil the fettuccine in a large pot of salted water. Drain when the pasta is *al dente* and pour into a heated dish. Serve with the simmering tomato sauce which will have reduced by this time. Then sprinkle with the coarsely chopped basil leaves.

Hint: Do not add cheese as it would overpower the delicate flavor of the fresh tomatoes and the aroma of the basil.

Fettuccine with lamb sauce

Time: 2½ hours
Ingredients:
1 lb fresh or dried fettuccine
8 lamb chops
a few cloves of garlic
a few sprigs of rosemary
  (or 1 tsp dried rosemary)
½ cup dry white wine
salt and pepper
4 to 5 tbsp olive oil
1 lb tomatoes, peeled and
  chopped or sliced

4 or 5 slices bacon
1 tbsp chopped parsley
1½ tbsp butter
2 oz (½ cup) grated Romano
  cheese

Using a sharp knife, make small incisions in the lamb chops and insert slivers of garlic and sprigs of rosemary. Put a little oil in a large saucepan and place the chops inside. Pour a little more oil over the meat, sprinkle with salt and pepper, cover with the bacon and place the pan over a high heat.

When the meat is well browned all over, pour the wine over and simmer until it evaporates. Then add the tomatoes, some parsley, and continue cooking over a gentle heat for about 1 hour.

When the chops are nearly cooked, boil the fettuccine in a large pot of salted water. Drain the pasta when it is *al dente*, and place in a serving dish. Add the butter (cut into pieces), some of the sauce from the lamb and the cheese. Arrange the chops on a large serving dish with the fettuccine in the center. Pour the rest of the hot sauce over both meat and pasta and serve.

Hint: The lamb chops may be cut from any part of the animal: the shoulder, rib, loin, or sirloin.

fettuccine with lamb sauce

Tagliatelle with lamb and curry sauce

Time: 1 hour 50 minutes
Ingredients:
1 lb fresh or dried tagliatelle
a shoulder of lamb weighing
*   about 2 lb*
a little olive oil
4 tbsp butter
1 shallot, chopped
a large pinch of curry powder
salt and pepper
1 cup heavy cream

Rinse and dry the lamb and cut into smallish pieces. Heat the oil with half the butter in a large pan and brown the lamb pieces. Add the chopped shallot, the curry powder, salt and pepper and pour in the cream. Cover the pan and simmer for about 1 hour on a very low heat.
Remove the lamb pieces from the sauce, strain the sauce and pour it back into the saucepan. Add the pieces of meat and simmer for a few minutes to reheat. Boil the tagliatelle in a large pot of salted water. Drain when the pasta is *al dente*. Stir in the butter, cut up, and some of the sauce. Pour the tagliatelle onto a preheated serving dish and arrange the meat around the edge, pouring the rest of the simmer-
ing sauce over the dish.
Hint: Serve as a main course. If you like exotic flavors, increase the quantity of curry powder. You can also add a pinch of saffron if you wish.

Pappardelle with rabbit

Time: 2 hours + marinating time for rabbit
Ingredients:
1 lb fresh or dried pappardelle
*   (or wide noodles)*
1 rabbit weighing about
*   2 1/2 lb, dressed*
2 cups full-bodied red wine
4 to 5 tbsp olive oil
1 large onion, sliced
2 stalks celery, chopped
3 carrots, chopped
1 clove garlic
2 juniper berries
a pinch of thyme
2 cloves
1 bay leaf
black peppercorns
salt
1 oz dried mushrooms
*   (or 1 lb fresh mushrooms)*
1 1/2 tbsp butter
1 slice bacon
a little flour
2 to 3 tbsp brandy
2 oz (1/2 cup) grated Parmesan
*   cheese*

pappardelle with rabbit

Rinse and cut the rabbit into small, similar-sized pieces and set aside the liver.

Put the meat in a dish and pour over the wine and a little oil. Add the sliced onion, one chopped stalk of celery and a carrot, the clove of garlic, juniper berries, thyme, cloves, bay leaf, a few peppercorns and salt, and let marinate for several hour or overnight.

Soak the dried mushrooms in water. Heat the butter and a little oil in a large pan and sauté the celery and carrots together with the chopped bacon. Drain and slice the mushrooms and, after a few minutes, add them to the other ingredients. Remove the pieces of rabbit from the marinade and drain. Flour lightly and arrange them in the pan with the vegetables. Add salt and, when the meat is well browned, pour in a little wine from the marinade together with the marinade vegetables, but remove the garlic.

Bring to a boil, cover and simmer for about 1 hour, over low heat, adding the rest of the wine if necessary. Ten minutes before removing the rabbit from the heat, add the liver. When the cooking is completed, remove the pieces of rabbit, discard the bay leaf and strain the sauce. Discard the vegetables, but purée the liver into the sauce. Bring the sauce to a boil again and add the brandy. Then remove the bones from the rabbit, put the meat back in the sauce and keep hot.

Boil the pappardelle in a large pot of salted water and drain when the noodles are *al dente*. Flavor the pasta with some of the sauce and cheese. Pour the pasta into a large, fairly deep serving dish and arrange the pieces of rabbit on and around the pasta.

Hint: Use cèpes-wood mushrooms if they are in season. If you have the time, allow the rabbit to marinate for two days.

Pappardelle au gratin

Time: 1 ½ hours
Ingredients:
*1 lb fresh or dried green
    pappardelle (or wide noodles)*
2 tbsp olive oil
4 oz bacon, chopped
1 small onion, chopped
1 carrot, chopped
1 stalk celery, chopped
1 spicy Italian sausage, chopped
salt and pepper
½ cup dry white wine
one 8-oz can peeled tomatoes

3 tbsp butter
4 tbsp flour
2 cups milk
a pinch of nutmeg
2 oz (¹/₂ cup) grated Parmesan
   cheese

Prepare the ragù: heat the oil and sauté the bacon, onion, carrot and celery. Add the sausage, salt and pepper. As soon as the sausage begins to brown, pour in the white wine which will evaporate. Force the tomatoes through a fine sieve, add them to the ragù and continue simmering over a gentle heat, stirring frequently and adding a little water or stock if necessary. Prepare the béchamel sauce: melt the butter and stir in the flour. Gradually pour in the milk; add salt and pepper and a little grated nutmeg to flavor. Simmer for almost 5 minutes, stirring constantly with a wooden spoon.
Preheat the oven to 350°F. Boil the pappardelle in a large pot of salted water and drain when the pasta is *al dente*. Pour into a large dish and cover with the ragù (leaving about 1 tbsp in the pan) and the cheese, and stir carefully. Spread the remaining ragù over the bottom of a baking dish and pour in the pasta.

Pour the béchamel over the pasta and put the dish in the oven until the surface is golden brown. Remove the dish from the oven and serve at once.
Hint: Rather than using canned tomatoes, substitute 2 lb fresh tomatoes, peeled and seeded.

Fusilli hunter's style

Time: 30 minutes
Ingredients:
1 lb fusilli
2 oz dried mushrooms
4 tbsp olive oil
1 small onion, finely chopped
1 stalk celery, finely sliced
1 clove garlic, finely chopped
4 slices bacon, diced
salt and pepper
4 to 6 tbsp dry white wine
2 oz smoked ham, diced
1 bay leaf

Soak the mushrooms in warm water. Heat the oil in a pan and sauté the onion, celery and garlic. As soon as they have browned, add the bacon, salt and pepper. Pour in the wine and when it has evaporated, add the drained mushrooms, ham and bay leaf and simmer for 15 minutes.
Boil the fusilli in a large pot of

— 81 —

salted water, drain when the pasta is *al dente* and remove the bay leaf from the sauce before pouring it over the fusilli.

Hint: To complete this rich Mediterranean meal, serve a salad of raw vegetables with a *pinzimonio* — an olive oil, pepper and salt dressing, and toasted whole-wheat bread.

Tasty maltagliati pie

Time: 1 hour
Ingredients:
1 lb maltagliati
   (diamond-shaped pasta)
2 tbsp olive oil
4 tbsp butter
1 small onion, chopped
1 carrot, chopped
1 stalk celery, chopped
4 oz ground beef
2 oz mortadella or bologna,
   chopped
2 oz ham, chopped
4 oz sausage meat, crumbled
salt
2 to 3 tbsp dry white wine
1 lb ripe tomatoes or one 8-oz
   can peeled tomatoes)
2 tbsp flour
1 cup milk
2 oz (1/2 cup) grated Parmesan
   cheese

In a large saucepan heat the oil and 2 tbsp of the butter and soften the onion, carrot and celery. Add the ground meat, the mortadella, ham and sausage. Brown thoroughly, add salt and sprinkle with the wine. Peel the tomatoes and force them through a fine sieve. When the wine has evaporated, add the tomatoes and continue simmering over low heat.

Melt the remaining butter in a saucepan and add the flour. Stir to remove any lumps and dilute with boiling milk, poured in a little at a time. Add salt and simmer for 5 minutes.

Boil the maltagliati in a large pot of salted water. Preheat the oven to 400°F. Drain the pasta when it is *al dente* and pour the tomato sauce over it, keeping back 2 or 3 tablespoons. Add half the cheese. Pour into a baking dish and cover with the béchamel sauce. Sprinkle the remaining tomato sauce and the rest of the Parmesan on top. Bake in the oven until the cheese has melted and the top is well browned.

Hint: Always preheat the oven to the required temperature before baking a dish. Most ovens take 15 to 20 minutes to reach a specific temperature.

Tagliatelle with veal kebabs

Time: 1 hour 45 minutes
Ingredients:
1 lb fresh or dried tagliatelle
1 lb veal
1 lb cherry tomatoes
a few sprigs of fresh sage
1 lemon
3 tbsp olive oil
salt and pepper
4 tbsp butter

Preheat the broiler to its highest setting. Cut the meat into large cubes and thread on skewers, with a tomato and a sage leaf between each piece of meat.

Squeeze the lemon and mix the juice with the olive oil, salt and pepper in a bowl.

Place the skewers on a baking tray and use a pastry brush to baste them with the oil and lemon mixture. Broil, basting and turning the skewers often.

Boil the tagliatelle in a large pot of salted water and drain when the pasta is *al dente*. Mix in the butter, cut up, and lots of freshly ground pepper. Arrange the skewers on top, pour the juices over the pasta and serve at once.

Hint: This makes an ideal main course as it contains pasta, meat and vegetables.

Tasty lasagna

Time: 1½ hours
Ingredients:
1 lb homemade or packaged
 lasagna noodles
1 lb spinach, washed
10 oz (1¼ cups) ricotta
a small bunch of fresh parsley
1 egg
2½ oz (⅔ cup) grated Parmesan
 cheese
salt and pepper
a pinch of nutmeg
4 tbsp butter
2 tbsp olive oil
1 small onion, chopped
1 small carrot, chopped
1 stalk celery, chopped
a bunch of fresh basil
4 oz ground beef
4 oz spicy Italian sausage,
 chopped
1 lb ripe tomatoes (or one 8-oz
 can peeled tomatoes)

Boil the spinach, drain and cut into strips. Force the ricotta through a sieve and combine with the spinach. Add the chopped parsley, half the Parmesan and the egg, and season with salt, pepper and nutmeg. Mix well to obtain a smooth paste.

Heat the butter and oil in a saucepan and sauté the onion, carrot, celery and basil, reserving a tablespoon of butter for later. Add the meat and the sausage and brown them. Force the tomatoes through a fine sieve and add them to the other ingredients in the pan. Season with salt and pepper and simmer for 40 minutes.

Preheat the oven to 350°F. Boil the lasagna, a few pieces at a time, in a large pot of salted water, drain when the pasta is *al dente* and spread on a clean cloth. Place a little spinach stuffing in the center of each piece of lasagna and roll the pasta up. Place the lasagna side by side in a buttered baking dish. Cover with the ragù, sprinkle the remaining cheese on top and bake for 15-20 minutes.

Hint: Remember to cook dried lasagna a few minutes longer than fresh.

Two-filling lasagna pie

Time: 1 hour 45 minutes
Ingredients:
1 lb homemade or packaged
  lasagna noodles
1 oz dried mushrooms
3 tbsp olive oil
2 oz lean bacon, chopped
1 small onion, chopped
8 oz lean ground beef
salt and pepper
2 chicken livers
1 tbsp tomato paste
1 tbsp flour
1 1/4 lb spinach, washed
4 oz ham, chopped
a pinch of nutmeg
1 egg
2 oz (1/2 cup) grated Parmesan
  cheese
3 1/2 tbsp butter

Soak the mushrooms in warm water. Heat the oil and sauté the bacon and onion; after a few minutes add the ground beef, salt and pepper, and brown the meat. Remove any greenish spots from the chicken livers, rinse and chop them and add to the other ingredients. Drain the mushrooms thoroughly and chop coarsely before adding them to the rest. Dilute the tomato paste with a little water and pour into the sauce; simmer over very low heat for about 45 minutes. When the mixture is almost ready, mix the flour with a little water and stir in.

Meanwhile, boil and chop the spinach and mix with the ham. Add the nutmeg, half the cheese, the egg and a pinch of salt. Mix to bind the ingredients. Preheat the oven to 350°F. Boil the lasagna, a few pieces at a time, in salted water, drain and dry on a cloth. Butter a baking dish and place a layer of lasagna on the bottom. Then make a layer of ragù sprinkled with Parmesan cheese, another layer of lasagna and then a layer of spinach filling. Continue alternating the layers until you have used up the ingredients, finishing with ragù. Put the dish in the oven and bake until there is a golden crust on the surface.

Hint: This should be served as a main course as it is very substantial.

Green lasagna with Bolognese sauce

Time: 1½ hours
Ingredients:
1 lb homemade or packaged
*   lasagna noodles*
1 oz dried mushrooms
1 small onion, chopped
4 tbsp butter
2 tbsp olive oil
8 oz ground beef
one 8-oz can peeled tomatoes
salt and pepper
4 tbsp flour
2 cups milk
a pinch of nutmeg
4 oz (1 cup) grated Parmesan
*   cheese*

Prepare the sauce: soak the mushrooms in warm water. Finely chop the onion and sauté in 1 tablespoon of the butter and the oil. Add the ground beef and brown. Drain and chop the mushrooms and add them to the pan. Simmer for 5 minutes before adding the tomatoes, salt and pepper. Simmer for a further 45 minutes.

Meanwhile, prepare the béchamel sauce: melt the remaining butter and stir in the flour. Boil the milk and stir it in, a little at a time. Add salt and heat the sauce for a few minutes, stirring continuously. Remove from the heat and flavor with nutmeg. Boil the lasagna, a few pieces at a time, in a large pot of salted water. Drain and lay the pieces out to dry on a clean towel.

Preheat the oven to a 375°F. Cover the bottom of a baking dish with a little ragù and place a round of lasagna (or a layer of rectangles) over it. Then make another layer of ragù, béchamel sauce and cheese. Continue alternating layers until you have used up the ingredients. The last layer should be ragù. Bake in the oven for 15-20 minutes.

Hint: You can prepare the same dish with either yellow or green pasta.

PASTA WITH
VEGETABLE SAUCES

Unlike ragù sauces, which are based on meat, vegetable
sauces are made from fresh vegetables and herbs.
The basic ingredient is nearly always tomatoes. The best
varieties to use are the little firm plum tomatoes with few
seeds. Other types may be substituted provided they are ripe
(though not over-ripe) and sweet. At times when fresh
tomatoes are not easy to find, canned ones may be used
instead. Other vegetables, whether mushrooms, eggplants,
zucchini, sweet peppers, artichokes, peas, beans or olives,
must be of good quality too.
To make a vegetable sauce, you nearly always start with a
soffritto, that is, a mixture of chopped aromatic vegetables
such as carrot, celery, onion or shallot, garlic and fresh
herbs, sautéed in olive oil, butter or other fat. It is useful
to remember that if the recipe does not specify what type of
fat to use a vegetable oil is preferable, especially
"extra virgin" (the best quality) olive oil, or high-grade
margarine.
All these elements are chosen, according to regional cooking
traditions, because in combination they make a harmonious
blend of tastes and colors.
There are also sauces where the predominant ingredients are
herbs, such as basil (used in the delicious Genoese *pesto*),
parsley, thyme, marjoram, rosemary, oregano and mint.
Where a herb plays the leading role in a sauce it must, of
course, be fresh; at other times it is possible to substitute
dried herbs when just a little of their flavor is required.
Among spices, spicy red chili peppers are often used in
vegetable sauces, either fresh, dried or ground.
The recipes that follow will serve 6 as a first course or 4 as
a main course.

Spaghetti with rosemary

Time: 20 minutes
Ingredients:
1 lb spaghetti
6 to 7 tbsp olive oil
1 clove garlic, crushed
a sprig of fresh rosemary or
1 tbsp crushed dried rosemary
one 10-oz can peeled tomatoes
salt

Heat the oil in a frying pan and add the garlic and rosemary. After a few minutes, add the tomatoes and simmer for a little longer.

Meanwhile, boil the spaghetti in a large pot of salted water for about 10 minutes and drain when the pasta is *al dente*.

Remove the garlic and the rosemary from the sauce and pour the sauce over the spaghetti.

Hint: This dish does not require grated Parmesan cheese and can be prepared in next to no time.

Spaghetti with eggplant and sweet pepper sauce

Time: 1 hour 50 minutes
Ingredients:
1 lb spaghetti
1 lb ripe tomatoes
6 tbsp olive oil
1 onion, sliced
1 carrot, chopped
1 stalk celery, chopped
1 tbsp chopped parsley
salt and pepper
2 1-lb eggplants
2 sweet bell peppers
1 tbsp capers
2 oz black olives, pitted
* and chopped*
a bunch of fresh basil

Blanch the tomatoes in boiling water, peel them, remove the seeds and chop the flesh. Heat 2 tablespoons of oil in a pan over a gentle heat and sauté the onion for several minutes, stirring from time to time. Cover the pan when you are not stirring. Add the chopped carrot, celery and parsley. Stir in the tomatoes, salt and pepper and simmer for about 1 hour over a low heat.

Meanwhile, dice the eggplants and sweet peppers. Arrange the eggplants on a large dish and salt them; tilt the dish and leave for about 1 hour so that any bitter liquid drains away. Dry the eggplant with paper towels and fry with the peppers in the remaining oil for about 10 minutes without adding any liquid.

Strain the tomato sauce and

spaghetti with eggplant and sweet pepper sauce

pour it back into its saucepan, adding the eggplants, peppers, capers and olives. Cover and simmer for another 20 minutes to blend all the flavors.

Boil the spaghetti in a large pot of salted water, drain and pour the sauce over the pasta. Chop the basil and sprinkle it over just before serving.

Hint: Other vegetables in season, such as zucchini or green beans, may be added.

Cold summer spaghetti

Time: 20 minutes
Ingredients:
1 lb very thin spaghetti
4 large ripe tomatoes, peeled,
  seeded and chopped
4 to 5 tbsp olive oil
2 tsp chopped fresh thyme
  or basil
salt and pepper

Put the tomato pieces in a bowl and pour in a little oil, add the thyme (or basil), freshly ground pepper and salt.

Boil the spaghetti in salted water, drain when the pasta is *al dente*, rinse under cold water to cool and pour into a dish. Pour the remaining oil over and mix in the tomatoes.

Hint: You can improvise with this sauce and add other appetizing ingredients such as capers, slices of olive, slivers of sweet pepper, chunks of tuna fish, and so on.

Ceriole with artichokes

Time: 45 minutes
Ingredients:
1 lb fresh ceriole
  (double pasta twists)
4 artichokes
1 small onion, chopped
1 stalk celery, finely chopped
1 clove garlic, finely chopped
4 tbsp olive oil
4 slices lean bacon, diced
1 lb ripe tomatoes, peeled,
  seeded and chopped
salt and pepper
3 to 4 tbsp white wine
2 oz smoked ham, chopped
1 bay leaf

Remove the artichokes' outer leaves and the hairy choke, wash and cut the artichokes into small pieces.

Sauté the chopped onion, celery and garlic in the oil, and as soon as the mixture begins to brown, add the bacon, the artichokes, the tomatoes, salt and pepper, and pour in the wine. As soon as

ceriole with artichokes

the wine has evaporated, add the ham and the bay leaf and simmer for another 15 minutes.

Boil the ceriole in a large pot of salted water, drain when the pasta is *al dente* and serve with the hot sauce, discarding the bay leaf first.

Hint: This "Mediterranean" pasta dish, which is rich and sustaining, should be served with a salad of raw vegetables with a dressing of olive oil, salt and pepper, and with toasted whole-wheat bread.

Macaroni with olives

Time: 40 minutes
Ingredients:
1 lb long smooth macaroni
1 clove garlic
1 chili pepper, fresh or dried
4 to 5 tbsp olive oil
salt
2 lb tomatoes, peeled, seeded
  and chopped
4 oz black oil-cured olives
1 tbsp capers
1 tbsp chopped parsley

Crush the garlic and chili pepper and sauté in the hot oil. Add the tomatoes together with salt; simmer for about 20 minutes. Remove the garlic and chili. Re-move the pits from the olives, chop the capers and add to the tomato sauce.

Break the macaroni into 3-inch lengths and boil in a large pot of salted water. Drain when the pasta is *al dente* and serve with the sauce. Garnish with the chopped parsley after having mixed well.

Hint: The sauce can be made without the tomatoes, just use more oil.

Macaroni baked in foil

Time: 30 minutes
Ingredients:
1 lb ribbed macaroni
1 lb ripe tomatoes, peeled
  and seeded
8 oz mozzarella cheese, diced
a bunch of fresh basil, chopped
2 tbsp butter, cut
  into slivers
salt and pepper

Cut the flesh of the tomatoes into strips and put in a bowl with the cubes of mozzarella, the fresh basil, the butter slivers and freshly ground pepper and mix well to make the sauce.

Boil the macaroni in a large pot of salted water and drain when the pasta is just *al dente* as it will

macaroni with olives

continue cooking in the oven. Add the pasta to the sauce and mix carefully.

Preheat the oven to 350°F, lay two sheets of aluminum foil on the work surface and divide the pasta between the two sheets, placing it in the center of each one. Fold up the sides to make a sealed packet and place on a baking tray. Bake in the oven for about 10 minutes. Transfer the foil parcels to a serving dish and unwrap the foil in front of everybody.

Hint: It is a good idea to adopt this method of cooking in aluminum foil because it requires little fat and allows the dish to retain its full flavor: during baking the aromas are sealed inside the foil envelope and absorbed by the pasta.

one 14-oz can peeled tomatoes
8 oz mozzarella cheese, diced

Heat 2 tablespoons of the oil in a saucepan, add the garlic and fry. Purée the tomatoes through a food mill and add to the pan, together with salt, pepper and sugar. Cover, turn down the heat and simmer for about 45 minutes.

Boil the macaroni in salted water and drain when the pasta is *al dente*. Pour into a dish and mix in the remaining oil at once, then stir in the anchovies and mozzarella. Pour the simmering sauce over the pasta and mix carefully.

Hint: Cut the mozzarella into very small pieces so that it melts as soon as it touches the hot pasta.

Macaroni with mozzarella and anchovies

Time: 1 hour
Ingredients:
1 lb very short ribbed macaroni
4 tbsp olive oil
1 clove garlic
salt and pepper
1 tsp sugar
2 oz anchovy fillets, drained
*   and chopped*

Penne with chili pepper

Time: 1 hour
Ingredients:
1 lb smooth penne
2 cloves garlic, crushed
5 to 6 tbsp olive oil
6 oz small mushrooms, washed
salt and pepper
a pinch of marjoram
1 1/2 lb tomatoes, peeled,
*   seeded and sliced*

macaroni with mozzarella and anchovies

3 tbsp dry white wine
1 fresh red chili pepper, sliced
2 oz (¹/₂ cup) grated Romano
cheese

Sauté the garlic in half the hot oil and add the mushrooms, whole. Add salt and pepper and simmer for a few minutes. Sprinkle with marjoram and pour in the wine. When the wine has evaporated, add the tomatoes and simmer for about 30 minutes, stirring from time to time.

Boil the penne in a large pot of salted water, drain when the pasta is *al dente* and transfer to a dish. Pour in more olive oil, add the tomato sauce, the sliced chili pepper and the Romano cheese. Mix well and serve at once.

Hint: If you don't like chili pepper, substitute slices of fresh sweet red pepper.

Rigatoni with aromatic herbs

Time: 1¹/₄ hours
Ingredients:
1 lb rigatoni (large ribbed
dried pasta tubes)
1 lb ripe tomatoes, peeled,
seeded and chopped
a pinch of sugar

salt and pepper
¹/₂ chili pepper, chopped
6 tbsp olive oil
a small bunch of arugula
(optional), chopped
a bunch of fresh parsley,
chopped
a bunch of fresh basil, chopped
1 tbsp each dry marjoram,
thyme, oregano, sage
and rosemary
1 oz (¹/₄ cup) grated Parmesan
cheese

Put the tomato pieces in a saucepan. Add the sugar, salt, pepper, chili pepper and two tablespoons of the oil.

Simmer the sauce for about 1 hour over low heat. Just before removing the saucepan from the heat, add all the herbs and stir.

Boil the rigatoni in a large pot of salted water, drain when the pasta is *al dente* and pour in the remaining olive oil. Sprinkle with Parmesan and pour half the sauce over the pasta. Mix well, garnish with the rest of the sauce and serve.

Hint: Always use fresh herbs when they are in season; they are much more aromatic. You can substitute other herbs for the ones in the recipe, depending on what is available in the shops or in your garden.

cannolicchi with ham and tomato sauce (p. 98)

Cannolicchi with ham and tomato sauce

Time: 40 minutes
Ingredients:
*1 lb cannolicchi (small
    dried pasta tubes)
4 to 5 tbsp olive oil
1 small onion, finely chopped
1 tbsp each fresh parsley
    and basil, chopped with
    1 clove garlic
4 oz smoked ham, finely
    chopped
1 1/4 lb fresh tomatoes, peeled,
    seeded and coarsely chopped
salt and pepper*

Heat the oil in a pan and sauté the onion, parsley, basil and garlic.
After a minute or two add the smoked ham and sauté until it turns pale.
Add the chopped tomatoes, salt and pepper and simmer for about 20 minutes.
Meanwhile, boil the cannolicchi in a large pot of salted water, drain when the pasta is *al dente* and serve with the boiling sauce. Sprinkle with a generous amount of chopped basil.
Hint: To finish the dish, you can add a handful of grated Parmesan cheese.

Trenette with zucchini sauce

Time: 40 minutes
Ingredients:
*1 lb trenette (thin noodles)
2 tbsp butter
4 to 5 tbsp olive oil
1 small onion, finely chopped
1 stalk celery, finely chopped
1 small carrot, finely chopped
2 lb ripe tomatoes, peeled,
    seeded and chopped
    (or one 10-oz can peeled
    tomatoes, chopped)
salt and pepper
1 egg
1 lb zucchini, trimmed,
    washed, then sliced
2 to 3 tbsp flour
2 oz (1/2 cup) grated Parmesan
    cheese*

Heat the butter and 2 tablespoons of oil in a pan and sauté the onion, celery and carrot, then add the tomatoes, salt and pepper. Cover the pan and simmer for about 30 minutes, stirring often.
Break the egg into a bowl and beat it. Dip the zucchini slices first in the egg and then in the flour and fry them in hot oil. Remove when they are golden brown and drain them on paper towels. Keep them hot.
Boil the trenette in a large pot of

ditaloni with eggplant (p. 100)

— 98 —

salted water. Drain when the pasta is *al dente*, place in a dish and pour the hot sauce over. Cover with the zucchini and grated Parmesan cheese. Mix and serve at once.

Hint: Cook this appetizing dish in the summer and when you can obtain new, sweet, tender zucchini.

Baked pasta-filled tomatoes

Time: 1 hour 40 minutes
Ingredients:
8 oz short ribbed macaroni
8 large ripe tomatoes,
    preferably all the same size
salt and pepper
1 ¹/₂ tbsp basil chopped
    with 1 clove garlic
4 to 5 tbsp olive oil
5 oz tomato paste

Slice the tops off the tomatoes horizontally and reserve them, remove and discard the seeds. Scoop out and reserve a little of the flesh, then turn the tomatoes upside-down on a plate to drain. Boil the pasta in salted water and remove it when it is just *al dente* — remember, it will continue to cook in the oven.
Preheat the oven to 350°F. In a bowl, mix the reserved tomato

flesh and about half the tomato paste with the chopped basil and garlic, salt and pepper and the boiled pasta. Mix carefully. Turn the tomatoes right side up, sprinkle a little salt and olive oil over them and fill them with the pasta mixture. Do not fill them by more than two-thirds. Arrange them in a baking dish and replace the tops on the tomatoes. Pour the rest of the tomato paste, diluted with a little water or, better still, stock, around the tomatoes.
Pour a little more oil over them and bake in the oven for about 40 minutes. Transfer the tomatoes to a heated plate and serve immediately, or serve them straight from the baking dish.

Hint: This is a new and interesting way of serving pasta. For the stuffing it is best to use types of small pasta which have a good "resistance" to cooking (they do not become overcooked easily).

Ditaloni with eggplant

Time: 1 ¹/₂ hours
Ingredients:
1 lb ribbed ditaloni (large
    dried pasta tubes)
salt and pepper

2 1-lb eggplants, washed
  and diced
4 tbsp olive oil
¹/₂ onion, sliced
¹/₂ tbsp chopped parsley
1 small carrot, chopped
1 stalk celery, chopped
1 lb ripe tomatoes, peeled,
  seeded and chopped
a bunch of fresh basil,
  chopped

Arrange the diced eggplant on a plate and add salt. Tilt the plate to allow the bitter juice to drain off and leave for 1 hour.

Meanwhile, prepare the sauce: heat two tablespoons of the oil in a pan and sauté the onion. Add the chopped parsley, carrot, celery, tomatoes, salt and pepper and stir well. Simmer for about 1 hour. You should obtain a thick sauce.

Dry the eggplant well (with paper towels) and fry in the remaining oil. Force the tomato sauce through a sieve and add the eggplant; simmer for another 15 minutes.

Meanwhile, boil the pasta in a large pot of salted water, drain when the pasta is *al dente* and serve with the sauce. Finish with the chopped basil.

Hint: Use only eggplants which are firm and not too big.

Cold ruote with tomato sauce

Time: 30 minutes
Ingredients:
1 lb ruote (dried pasta wheels)
10 oz tomatoes, peeled
  and seeded
salt and pepper
3 tbsp olive oil
1 tbsp parsley, chopped
  with 1 clove garlic
1 tbsp chopped basil

Cut the flesh of the tomatoes into small pieces. Purée in a food mill, blender, or food processor. Boil the pasta in a large pot of salted water, drain and cool under cold running water. Drain once more and pour into a deep dish. Pour a little oil over the pasta at once. Add salt and pepper to the tomato sauce and pour it over the pasta, stirring well. Sprinkle with the parsley, garlic, basil, a little pepper and the remaining oil and serve cold.

Hint: Serve in summer when ripe, flavorful tomatoes are easy to obtain.

Ruote with olives and capers

Time: 40 minutes

Ingredients:

1 lb ruote (dried pasta wheels)
1 sweet green bell pepper
1 small onion, chopped
2¹/₂ oz smoked bacon, diced
2 tbsp olive oil
1 lb ripe tomatoes, peeled,
   seeded and chopped
2 oz each green and black olives,
   pitted and sliced
a pinch of oregano
1 tbsp capers
salt and pepper

Hold the pepper on the end of a fork over a gas flame to blister the skin. Rub with a cloth to remove the skin. Then, cut the pepper open, remove the seeds and cut the flesh into strips.

Sauté the onion and bacon in a little hot oil; when the bacon begins to brown, add the strips of pepper and let them soften. Then add the tomatoes, the olives, the oregano, the capers and a little salt and pepper. Simmer the sauce for about 20 minutes or until it thickens.

Boil the ruote in a large pot of salted water, drain when the pasta is *al dente* and serve with the hot sauce.

Hint: Do not add cheese to this dish. This sauce goes equally well with other types of short pasta, such as fusilli and conchiglie.

Tagliatelle with tomato and herb sauce

Time: 1¹/₂ hours
Ingredients:

1 lb fresh or dried tagliatelle
2 lb very ripe tomatoes,
   peeled and seeded
a pinch of thyme
2 bay leaves
a pinch of sugar
4 tbsp olive oil
salt

Crush the tomatoes and put them in a saucepan. Add a few pinches of salt, the thyme, bay leaves and sugar, and simmer until the sauce has reduced and thickened. Then, force it through a sieve and remove the bay leaves. Mix in 2 tablespoons of olive oil when the cooking is over.

Boil the tagliatelle in a large pot of salted water, drain when the pasta is *al dente* and pour into a dish. Pour the remaining olive oil over the tagliatelle followed by the tomato sauce.

Hint: This delicate pasta dish is particularly suitable for those with sensitive stomachs, as the sauce is simple and made without a *soffritto* (base of sautéed onions, celery and carrot).

tagliatelle with tomato and herb sauce

Tagliatelle with cheesy onion sauce

Time: 45 minutes
Ingredients:
1 lb fresh or dried tagliatelle
6 tbsp butter
1 lb onions, sliced
1 tbsp flour
4 oz (1 cup) shredded Gruyère
cheese
2 cups milk
salt

Heat 4 tbsp of the butter in a pan. Add the onions, cover and cook over low heat for about 20 minutes. The onion should cook, but not brown. Stir frequently. Mix in the flour and cook for a few more minutes.

Stir in the Gruyère, mix well and dilute by pouring in the milk a little at a time. Bring to a boil, add salt and simmer, stirring constantly, for about 10 minutes. Boil the tagliatelle in a large pot of salted water, drain when the pasta is *al dente* and pour into a preheated dish containing the remaining butter, cut in pieces. Mix carefully, cover with the onion sauce and serve at once.

Hint: If they have a too strong flavor, the onions can be blanched in boiling salted water for a few minutes before slicing.

Green tagliatelle with mushrooms and peas

Time: 1 hour 45 minutes
Ingredients:
1 lb fresh or dried green
tagliatelle
3 tbsp olive oil
2 tbsp butter
½ small onion, finely chopped
4 oz smoked ham or bacon,
half fat and half lean, finely
chopped
6 oz mushrooms, washed
and sliced
salt and pepper
1 lb fresh tomatoes, peeled
and put through a food mill
1 cup fresh or frozen peas
2 oz (½ cup) grated Parmesan
cheese

Heat the olive oil and half the butter in a pan and sauté the onion and ham. Add the mushrooms, salt and pepper and, after 5 minutes, the tomatoes. Simmer over low heat, stirring frequently.

Boil the peas separately in a little water or, better still, stock, and add them 10 minutes before removing the pan from the stove. Boil the tagliatelle in salted water, drain when the pasta is *al dente* and pour it into a soup tureen that has been warmed by having boiling water poured into it, and then dried. Pour the mushroom and pea sauce over the tagliatelle and stir in the remaining butter and the cheese.

Hint: Use fresh peas when in season; they are sweeter and more delicate in flavor.

Fazzoletti with basil cream sauce

Time: 30 minutes
Ingredients:
1 lb fazzoletti (small squares
  of fresh egg pasta) or
  packaged lasagna noodles
a large bunch of fresh basil
1 or 2 cloves garlic
1 cup heavy cream
2 oz (¹/₂ cup) grated Parmesan
  cheese
salt and white pepper
2 tbsp butter

Wash and dry the basil leaves, and purée them in the blender with the garlic and a few tablespoons of heavy cream; this should give you a soft, smooth cream. Make a similar paste with the cheese and a few more tablespoons of cream by processing them in the blender for a few seconds.
Boil the fazzoletti in a large pot

of salted water. Meanwhile, heat the butter with the remaining cream and add the cheese mixture. Drain the pasta when it is *al dente*, pour it into a dish and add the cheese sauce and, finally, the basil mixture. Mix carefully and serve.

Hint: Make lots of basil cream and serve some of it separately in a sauceboat. It is good with gnocchi as well.

Homemade lasagna with pesto

Time: 1¹/₄ hours
Ingredients:
For the pasta
3¹/₂ cups hard-wheat flour
  (semolina)
6 "large" eggs
salt
For the sauce
8 oz fresh basil
2 cloves garlic
1 tbsp pine nuts
a pinch of marjoram
2 oz (¹/₂ cup) grated Parmesan
  cheese
¹/₄ cup olive oil
salt

Prepare the egg pasta as described on page 21. Roll out the dough very thinly and, using a pastry wheel, cut out rounds which are slightly smaller in diameter than the dish in which you intend to serve the pasta. Arrange the rounds of pasta on the floured pastry board.

Wash the basil leaves, drain, dry and chop them together with the garlic and the pine nuts. Put the mixture in a bowl and add the marjoram, cheese, and a pinch of salt, then slowly pour in the oil. Mix again.

Boil the rounds of pasta, one at a time, for a few minutes, in salted water. Drain and dry them with a towel and arrange them in a warmed serving dish, alternating each layer with a layer of basil sauce.

Hint: To save time, make the basil sauce in a blender and add 2 or 3 extra tablespoons of oil.

Baked macaroni

Time: 45 minutes
Ingredients:
1 lb short ribbed macaroni
10 oz mushrooms
1 clove garlic
2 tbsp olive oil
³/₄ cup tomato sauce
salt and pepper
4 tbsp butter
2 oz (¹/₂ cup) grated Parmesan cheese
4 oz (¹/₂ cup) Fontina cheese
4 oz lean ham, diced
2 eggs, beaten

Wipe the mushrooms and slice them thinly. Brown the whole clove of garlic in the oil and add the mushrooms. Sauté them and then add the tomato sauce; simmer until the mushrooms are cooked.

Meanwhile, boil the macaroni in a large pot of salted water. Drain when the pasta is al *dente*. Preheat the oven to 350°F. Put three tablespoons of the butter, cut up, into the bottom of a baking dish with the Parmesan and Fontina cheeses and the ham. Mix well, add the macaroni and a little of the water it was cooked in. Pour in the beaten eggs, add pepper and mix again. Dot with the remaining butter. Bake in the oven for 15-20 minutes.

Remove the clove of garlic from the mushroom and tomato sauce and serve with the baked pasta.

Hint: This dish contains eggs, cheese and ham, making it a substantial meal. A salad of raw vegetables is recommended to complete the menu.

baked macaroni

Tagliatelle soufflé

Time: 1 hour
Ingredients:
10 oz fresh or dried tagliatelle
salt and pepper
6 cups milk
4 tbsp butter
2 eggs

Boil the tagliatelle in the lightly salted milk.

Meanwhile, beat the butter with a spoon until it is creamy and add the egg yolks one at a time, a pinch of pepper and about 1 cup of boiling milk.

Preheat the oven to 350°F.

Drain the tagliatelle when the pasta is *al dente* and pour the pasta into the dish containing the beaten egg yolks. Beat the egg whites until stiff and fold them into the other ingredients. Butter a baking dish and pour in the tagliatelle mixture. Bake until the surface begins to brown — about 30-40 minutes. Remove from the oven, let cool for a few minutes and serve.

Hint: To test whether the soufflé is cooked all the way through, plunge a toothpick or knife blade into the center; the filling should be set and not still liquid.

Malloreddus with tomato sauce

Time: 1 hour 50 minutes
Ingredients:
1 lb fresh or dried malloreddus
2 oz bacon, chopped
1 small onion, sliced
4 tbsp olive oil
1 clove garlic, crushed
a few basil leaves
2 lb fresh tomatoes, peeled, seeded and chopped
½ beef bouillon cube
salt and pepper
2½ oz (⅔ cup) grated Romano cheese

Soften the bacon and onion in the hot oil. Add the garlic, basil and, after a few minutes, the tomatoes.

Dissolve the bouillon cube in a little water and add to the pan with the salt and pepper.

Simmer until a thick sauce is obtained.

Boil the malloreddus in a large pot of salted water, drain when the pasta is *al dente* and serve with the hot sauce and the cheese.

Hint: If you are using dried pasta, add a tiny pinch of saffron to the water to brighten the color.

malloreddus with tomato sauce

Homemade cappieddi with mushroom sauce

Time: 1½ hours
Ingredients:
For the pasta
*3½ cups hard-wheat flour
    (semolina)
6 "large" eggs
a pinch of salt*
For the sauce
*4 tbsp olive oil
1 medium-sized onion, finely
    sliced
2 oz smoked ham, diced
1 clove garlic
10 oz fresh mushrooms
14 oz fresh or canned
    peeled tomatoes
a bunch of fresh basil
a bunch of fresh parsley
salt and pepper
2 oz (½ cup) grated Parmesan
    cheese*

Mix the flour, eggs and salt into a dough as described on page 21. Roll out the dough in a thin sheet and, using a serrated pastry wheel or a knife, cut out little squares. Fold them in half, diagonally, making each one look like a little hat. Lay them out on the pastry board to dry, keeping them well apart.
Heat the oil in a pan and soften the onion, ham and whole clove of garlic. Wipe the mushrooms with a damp cloth, cut off the base of the stalks, slice them and add to the pan; simmer for a few minutes. Then add the tomatoes. Tie the bunches of basil and parsley together with kitchen string before putting them into the pan with the other ingredients. Add salt and freshly ground pepper. Simmer for 35-40 minutes.
Boil the pasta in a large pot of salted water, drain when it is *al dente*, transfer to a serving dish and pour the sauce over it. Remove the herbs and the garlic and serve with the cheese.
Hint: To save time, use commercial dried farfalle instead of homemade cappieddi.

Trofie with basil sauce

Time: 1 ½ hours
Ingredients:
*1 lb fresh trofie
2 bunches of fresh basil
1 clove garlic
1 tbsp pine nuts
salt
½ cup olive oil
1 tbsp grated Romano cheese
1 tbsp grated Parmesan cheese*

Wash the basil leaves and lay

trofie with basil sauce

them on a towel to dry. Then put them in a mortar with the garlic, pine nuts and a pinch of salt. Crush against the bottom and sides of the mortar with the pestle until you obtain a paste. Add the oil, a little at a time, and finally, combine the Romano and the Parmesan cheeses and add them to the mixture. Boil the trofie in a large pot of salted water, drain when *al dente* and serve at once with a generous amount of sauce.

Hint: You can vary the basil sauce by adding crushed walnuts or a pinch of Cayenne pepper.

Spaghetti with zucchini blossoms and basil

Time: 40 minutes
Ingredients:
1 lb thin spaghetti
1 lb ripe tomatoes
1 small white onion, sliced
1 clove garlic
3 to 4 tbsp olive oil
about 10 very fresh zucchini
  blossoms, pistils removed,
  washed and coarsely sliced
salt and pepper
a few basil leaves

Blanch the tomatoes in boiling water, peel and put them through a food mill. Soften the onion and the whole clove of garlic in the hot oil and add the zucchini blossoms. Fry until they wilt and then add the tomatoes and whole basil leaves and continue cooking until the sauce has thickened. At the end, discard the garlic and basil leaves.

Boil the spaghetti in a large pot of salted water, drain when the pasta is *al dente*, pour into a dish and add the sauce. Mix with care, add pepper and garnish with a few basil leaves.

Hint: Do not add cheese as this would smother the delicate flavor of the fresh flowers.

Whole-wheat spaghetti with vegetable sauce

Time: 30 minutes
Ingredients:
1 lb whole-wheat spaghetti
1 small onion, finely chopped
1 clove garlic, finely chopped
4 or 5 tbsp olive oil
$1/2$ sweet red or yellow
  bell pepper
12 oz fresh or canned peeled
  tomatoes
salt and pepper
4 oz stuffed olives, sliced
1 tbsp chopped parsley

spaghetti with zucchini blossoms and basil

Sauté the onion and garlic in the hot oil. Char the sweet pepper over a flame and peel off the skin. Slice the flesh and sauté with the onion for a few minutes. Then add the tomatoes, salt, pepper and the sliced olives (reserving a few for garnish). Continue simmering, stirring from time to time. Before removing the sauce from the stove, add the parsley.

Boil the spaghetti, drain when the pasta is *al dente* and serve with the sauce.

Hint: This type of sauce doesn't require the addition of cheese.

Whole-wheat spaghetti with anchovies and capers

Time: 30 minutes
Ingredients:
1 lb whole-wheat spaghetti
5 to 6 tbsp olive oil
1 tbsp chopped parsley
1 clove garlic, chopped
a few anchovy fillets in oil,
  drained and cut into strips
10 oz ripe tomatoes, chopped
1 tbsp tomato paste
salt and pepper
1 tbsp capers, rinsed and sliced

Heat the oil in a saucepan. Add the chopped parsley, garlic and anchovies and sauté over low heat. Add the tomato pieces to the pan, dilute the tomato paste and pour in, and season with salt and pepper. When the sauce thickens, add the capers and let simmer for a few minutes more. Boil the pasta in a large pot of salted water, drain when it is *al dente* and serve with the sauce.

Hint: You can garnish the dish with additional anchovy fillets.

Macaroni with garlic, oil and chili pepper

Time: 20 minutes
Ingredients:
1 lb long smooth macaroni
salt
1/2 cup olive oil
3 cloves garlic, crushed
1 fresh chili pepper
a small bunch of fresh parsley

Divide the macaroni into pieces about 4 inches long, boil in salted water and drain when the pasta is *al dente*. Heat the oil and sauté the garlic. Stir in the chili pepper and cook briefly so the oil absorbs the flavors. Pour the sauce over the macaroni, sprinkle with the parsley, mix and serve.

Hint: This very quick dish is also good cold.

macaroni with garlic, oil and parsley

PASTA WITH
FISH SAUCES

Fresh fish, shellfish, good quality olive oil, white and black pepper and many different herbs are the basic ingredients for fish sauces.

It is essential to start with a *soffritto* (sautéed mixture) of garlic or onion in oil, and to add natural aromatic herbs and spices. The most commonly used are parsley, basil, oregano, mint and thyme.

There are many different fish sauces — cooked or uncooked, with or without tomatoes — all equally appetizing and quick to make. All that is required is a balanced choice of ingredients. The secrets for an excellent sauce are few but essential: very fresh fish, preferably straight from the water (molluscs that are still alive), fresh herbs and the appropriate pasta, should be used. No part of the fish should be wasted; the water inside shellfish as well as the *fumet* (the liquid obtained by poaching fish scraps or shells in water and wine) can be added to the sauce (after boiling to reduce it and straining) to enhance the flavor.

Note that while we have spoken only of fresh fish, frozen fish is an excellent substitute when fresh fish is out of season or unavailable at your local store. In fact, since frozen fish is frozen as soon as it is caught, it may be even better than fresh fish of dubious origin.

Long dried pasta shapes are recommended with fish sauces, for example, bucatini, spaghetti, zite, macaroni and fusilli.

The recipes that follow will serve 6 as a first course or 4 as a main course.

Fusilli with eels

Time: 1 ½ hour
Ingredients:
10 oz fusilli
10 oz tiny eels
4 tbsp flour
4 tbsp olive oil
1 small onion, chopped
1 clove garlic (optional)
2 lb fresh young peas
salt and pepper
3 to 4 tbsp dry white wine
1 lb ripe tomatoes, peeled,
  seeded and chopped
1 tbsp chopped parsley

Gut the eels and cut into pieces without removing the skin. Wash, dry and flour the pieces. Heat the olive oil and sauté the onion. Add a whole clove of garlic if you wish. Add the peas and simmer for about 10 minutes, adding a little water. Put in the eel pieces, salt and pepper, and brown them. After a few minutes, pour in the white wine and simmer until it has almost evaporated. At this point add the tomatoes and a little water. Simmer, stirring from time to time, until both the peas and the fish are tender and cooked through.
Ten minutes before removing the eels from the heat, boil the fusilli in a large pot of salted water, drain when the pasta is *al dente* and pour a little of the sauce over it. Pour the pasta into the middle of a deep serving dish, arrange the eels around the edge, add the rest of the sauce and garnish with parsley.
Hint: Serve as a main course followed simply by a selection of cheeses.

Bucatini with hake

Time: 45 minutes
Ingredients:
1 lb bucatini
1 hake weighing about 1 lb
4 tbsp olive oil
1 small onion, chopped
salt and pepper
3 to 4 tbsp dry white wine
10 oz peeled tomatoes, forced
  through a sieve
1 tbsp parsley chopped with
  1 clove garlic

Gut the hake, make a lengthwise cut and, using a sharp pointed knife, fillet the fish. Wash and dry thoroughly with paper towels.
Heat the oil in a frying pan and sauté the onion. Cut the hake fillets into pieces before adding them to the pan. Add salt and

fusilli with eels

pepper and brown the fish. Pour a few tablespoons of white wine over and allow it to evaporate. Then add the tomatoes and simmer gently, until the sauce thickens.

Meanwhile, boil the bucatini in a large pot of salted water and drain when the pasta is *al dente*. Pour into a deep dish. Add the chopped parsley to the sauce at the last moment and pour over the bucatini.

Hint: Do not serve any kind of cheese with this dish, not even mild varieties.

Bucatini alla marinara

Time: 1¼ hours
Ingredients:
1 lb bucatini
1 oz dried mushrooms
1 clove garlic
a few sage leaves
⅓ cup olive oil
1 onion, chopped
1 carrot, chopped
1 stalk celery, chopped
½ cup dry white wine
4 oz squid, cut into
   small pieces
4 oz shrimp
¼ cup brandy
a tiny pinch of saffron
½ tsp curry powder

14 oz canned peeled tomatoes
4 oz shelled mussels
4 oz shelled clams
1 tbsp chopped parsley
salt and pepper

Soak the mushrooms in warm water.

Sauté the garlic and sage leaves in the hot oil; remove them and put in the onion, carrot and celery and soften for a couple of minutes. Add the white wine and allow it to evaporate. Drain the mushrooms and add them, together with the squid pieces. Simmer over low heat for about 10 minutes, then add the shrimp and the brandy. Dissolve the saffron and curry powder in a little of the sauce and add them to the other ingredients together with the tomatoes. Cover the pan and simmer until the sauce thickens.

About 10 minutes before removing the pan from the heat, add the mussels and clams. Season the sauce to taste and, finally, sprinkle with chopped parsley.

Boil the bucatini in a large pot of salted water, drain when the pasta is *al dente* and pour on half the sauce. Arrange on a serving dish and pour on the rest of the sauce.

Hint: Add the shellfish at the last

minute and avoid overcooking them; otherwise they will become rubbery. Keep some of the water from the mussels and clams, and add it to the sauce to enhance the flavor.

Maritime spaghetti

Time: 1½ hours
Ingredients:
1 lb spaghetti
1 lb fresh clams
5 tbsp olive oil
2 cloves garlic, finely chopped
1 lb ripe tomatoes or one
  8-oz can tomatoes, peeled
  and forced through a sieve
salt and pepper
8 oz octopus or squid, cleaned
  and thinly sliced
8 oz shrimp, peeled
1½ tbsp chopped parsley

Scrub the clams and heat them in a small frying pan over moderate heat to open the shells. Remove the clams from the shells as they open and reserve the liquid that collects in the pan.
Heat 2 tablespoons of the oil and sauté the garlic. Add the tomatoes, salt and freshly ground pepper and let the sauce simmer until it thickens.
In a separate saucepan, heat the rest of the oil, put in the octopus or squid slices, salt and pepper, and cook for about 15 minutes. Then add the shrimp to the octopus. Strain the liquid from the clams and add to the octopus and shrimp. Continue simmering. Just before removing the sauce from the heat, add the clams to the pan.
Boil the spaghetti in a large pot of salted water and drain when the pasta is *al dente*. Place in a warmed serving dish and pour the tomato sauce over the pasta. Then pour on the fish with their sauce. Sprinkle generously with chopped parsley.
Hint: Do not serve cheese with this dish. If necessary, add a little dry white wine to the octopus or squid during cooking.

Spaghetti with squid

Time: 1¼ hours
Ingredients:
1 lb spaghetti
4 to 6 large squid
5 to 6 tbsp olive oil
salt
1 small onion, finely chopped
1 clove garlic, finely chopped
a bunch of fresh parsley,
  chopped
Cayenne pepper

1 carrot, finely chopped
1 stalk celery, finely chopped
1 lb ripe tomatoes or one
   8-oz can peeled tomatoes,
   forced through a sieve

Pull off the heads of the squid, remove the transparent backbone, and squeeze out the jelly-like viscera. Wash well. Peel off the outer skin and cut the flesh into thin slices.

Heat the oil and add the chopped onion, carrot, celery, garlic and half the parsley. Sauté, then add the squid slices, salt, a generous pinch of Cayenne pepper and the tomatoes. Cover and simmer over low heat until the squid is tender.

Boil the spaghetti in a large pot of salted water, drain when the pasta is *al dente*, add the sauce and sprinkle the remaining parsley on top.

Hint: If the sauce thickens too much before the squid are cooked, add a little water or dry white wine.

Spaghetti with mussels

Time: 1 hour
Ingredients:
1 lb spaghetti
2 cloves garlic, crushed
2 lb fresh mussels
   (or 8-oz bottled or frozen
   mussels)
4 tbsp olive oil
12 oz fresh or canned peeled
   tomatoes
salt and pepper
a large bunch of fresh parsley,
   chopped

Scrub the mussels thoroughly under running water, drain well and place in a large frying pan over moderate heat. Leave until they open, stirring occasionally with a wooden spoon. Put a few mussels to one side and remove the others from their shells.

Strain the liquid which has collected in the pan (it will have a 'sea' flavor) through a sieve lined with a piece of cheesecloth, and reserve the liquid.

Boil the spaghetti in a large pot of salted water. Meanwhile, sauté the garlic in the oil. When it begins to brown, add the liquid from the mussels, the tomatoes, salt and pepper. Boil over high heat until the sauce thickens. Then add the clams, stir, and remove from the heat.

Drain the spaghetti when it is *al dente*, pour into a warmed serving dish and serve with the mussel sauce. Sprinkle the chopped parsley on top and garnish with

spaghetti with mussels

the mussels in their shells set aside earlier.

Hint: If you use bottled mussels (but not mussels in vinegar), add the liquid they come in to the sauce, even though the flavor will not be so strong. You can also make the mussel sauce without tomatoes, using a little more oil.

Bucatini with shrimp and clams

Time: 1 1/4 hours
Ingredients:
1 lb bucatini
1 lb raw or cooked shrimp
1 bay leaf
2 lb clams
3 tbsp brandy
1 small onion, chopped
1 clove garlic, chopped
4 tbsp olive oil
14 oz tomatoes, peeled
  and chopped
salt and pepper

If the shrimp are raw boil them in a little water with the bay leaf. Heat the clams in a frying pan to open the shells and, as they open, remove the clams from the shells and reserve the liquid that has collected in the bottom of the frying pan.

Peel the shrimp and keep both their cooking water and their shells. Mix the strained cooking liquid from the clams with that from the shrimp. Crush the shrimp shells and add them, together with the brandy. Reduce the fish stock over a high heat for about 15 minutes and strain through a sieve lined with cheesecloth.

Fry the onion and garlic in 2 tablespoons of the oil and add the tomato. Pour in the strained fish stock, add salt and pepper and simmer over moderate heat until the sauce thickens.

Meanwhile, boil the bucatini in a large pot of salted water. Add the clams and shrimp to the sauce and allow the flavors to blend for a few minutes. Drain the pasta when it is *al dente* and serve with the remaining oil and the piping hot sauce.

Hint: Shellfish are generally added to the sauce at the last minute; otherwise, if they are overcooked, they become hard and rubbery.

Linguine with mussel sauce

Time: 1 1/4 hours
Ingredients:
1 lb linguine

bucatini with shrimp and clams

2 lb mussels
¹/₂ cup dry white wine
3 tbsp olive oil
1 shallot or small onion,
  chopped
1 clove garlic, chopped
a 1-inch piece of fresh chili
  pepper sliced
1 lb ripe tomatoes, peeled
  and put through a food mill
1 tbsp capers
salt and pepper
a bunch of parsley, chopped

Scrub the mussels and wash them thoroughly under running water. Put them in a large frying pan, pour on the wine and heat until the shells open. Remove the mussels from their shells and set them aside together with the liquid which collected in the bottom of the pan. Reduce and strain this liquid.

Heat the oil and soften the shallot, garlic and chili pepper. After a few minutes, add the tomato, capers, salt and pepper and continue to simmer over high heat. Five minutes before the sauce is reduced enough to be removed from the heat, add the liquid from the mussels and then the mussels. Simmer for 2 minutes, remove from the heat and add the chopped parsley.

Boil the linguine in a large pot of salted water, drain when the pasta is *al dente* and serve with the sauce.

Hint: Do not serve cheese with this dish. To ensure that the mussels are fresh and alive, check that the shells are either firmly closed or only slightly open. If one is slightly open, it should snap shut when touched. Discard any mussels that do not close. Similarly, after heating the mussels in the frying pan, discard any that have not opened.

Macaroni with shrimp

Time: 1¹/₄ hours
Ingredients:
1 lb long smooth macaroni
a sprig of fresh parsley
1 bay leaf
1 stalk celery
a few peppercorns
salt
2 lb large raw shrimp
¹/₃ cup olive oil
1 or 2 cloves garlic
a 1-inch piece of fresh chili
  pepper, shredded
1¹/₄ lb ripe tomatoes, peeled,
  seeded and chopped
1 tbsp chopped parsley

Fill a large saucepan with water and add the sprig of parsley, the bay leaf, celery, peppercorns and salt and bring to a boil. Wash the shrimp and immerse them in the boiling water for 3 to 4 minutes. Drain, and remove the transparent shells. Reserve a few unpeeled shrimp for garnish, and cut the rest into pieces. Break the macaroni into 4-inch lengths (or longer if you prefer) and boil in a large pot of salted water.

Heat the oil and brown the whole cloves of garlic. Add the chili, tomatoes and salt; simmer for 10 to 15 minutes until the sauce has thickened. Add the shrimp and continue simmering for a very short time.

Drain the macaroni when the pasta is *al dente*, pour the sauce over the macaroni and transfer to a serving dish. Sprinkle with the chopped parsley. Garnish with the whole shrimp.

Hint: To enhance the flavor of the sauce, press the shrimp shells against a sieve with the back of a spoon and add the result, even though there may not be much, to the sauce.

Torciglioni with tuna

Time: 30 minutes
Ingredients:
1 lb torciglioni (dried pasta twists)
1 clove garlic, crushed
5 to 6 tbsp olive oil
3¹/₃ oz canned tuna in oil, mashed with a fork
10 oz fresh tomatoes, peeled and forced through a sieve
salt and pepper
a pinch of oregano

Sauté the garlic in the oil over moderate heat. Remove the garlic and put in the tuna and, after a few minutes, the tomato. Add salt and oregano and continue simmering until the sauce thickens.

Meanwhile, boil the torciglioni in a large pot of salted water, drain when the pasta is *al dente* and serve with the tuna sauce, seasoned with plenty of freshly ground pepper.

Hint: To make a lighter dish, use less oil and drain the oil from the canned tuna.

Penne with smoked salmon

Time: 30 minutes
Ingredients:
1 lb penne
1 tbsp butter
1¹/₂ tbsp flour
1 cup milk, boiled
5 oz smoked salmon, sliced

4 oz (1 cup) grated Parmesan
  cheese
²/₃ cup cream
salt

Melt the butter in a saucepan and add the flour, stirring well. Add the hot milk, little by little, to obtain a smooth béchamel sauce. Remove from the heat and stir in the Parmesan cheese and the cream. Allow to cool. Force half the salmon through a sieve and stir it into the sauce.

Boil the penne in salted water and drain when the pasta is *al dente*. Meanwhile preheat the oven 350°F. Pour the penne into a baking dish and cover with the salmon sauce. Top with the remaining salmon slices and put in the oven for about 10 minutes.

Hint: Fish does not always go well with cheese. In this case, however, you can combine them as the delicate flavor of the sophisticated sauce will not be spoiled.

Macaroni with sardines

Time: 1 hour
Ingredients:
1 lb macaroni
3 tbsp raisins
1 lb fresh sardines

1 onion, chopped
¹/₃ cup olive oil
4 anchovy fillets, crushed
  to a paste
a pinch of fennel seeds
a pinch of saffron
3 tbsp pine nuts
2 tbsp butter

Soak the raisins in warm water. Rinse, cut open and remove the bones from the sardines.

Sauté the onion in half the oil and add half the sardines and the anchovy paste. Stir, and add the fennel seeds and saffron. Drain the raisins and add to the other ingredients together with the pine nuts and a little water to make a sauce which is not too thick. Stir the sauce to blend the ingredients. Fry the remaining sardines in the rest of the oil until they are golden brown. Preheat the oven to 350°F.

Boil the macaroni in a large pot of salted water, drain when the pasta is *al dente* and add half the sauce. Butter a baking dish and pour in the macaroni. Top with the fried sardines and pour on the rest of the sauce. Place in the oven for about 10 minutes.

Hint: The raisins make this a rather unusual recipe; if they do not appeal to your taste you can omit them.

macaroni with sardines

PASTA WITH
WHITE SAUCES

White sauces for pasta are made with few rich ingredients: butter, milk, cream and cheese with the occasional addition of egg yolks. Their hallmark is delicacy of flavor. Tomatoes and herbs, with few exceptions, are set aside to make way for fresh cheeses like mozzarella, ricotta and mascarpone, matured cheeses like Parmesan and other hard or semihard cheeses such as Fontina, Gruyère and Emmenthal. They are always added (the soft and semi-hard cheeses, that is) cut into tiny slivers or shredded so that they will melt easily in a *bain-marie* or double boiler over a low heat.

Olive oil plays a minor role too and is replaced by top quality fresh butter and cream. The cream most recommended for these sauces is heavy cream. It should be added at the last minute so that it will blend perfectly with the other ingredients.

Other special ingredients include nuts, delicate meats and shellfish, spices and, as an ultimate luxury, the rare fragrance of truffles. Not all the sauces in this section are necessarily "white" in color, nor is the term "white" sauce synonymous of "light" in texture. Classic "white sauces" of milk and cream added to a roux base of butter and flour are described as béchamel sauces throughout this book.

These same ingredients which give them their special designation of "white", however, are also much richer in fats than vegetable sauces or ragus.

White sauces are ideal for pasta made with eggs or homemade green pasta but it is equally good with pastas, like ravioli or tortelloni, stuffed with vegetables.

The recipes that follow will serve 6 as a first course or 4 as a main course.

Four-flavored spaghetti

Time: 40 minutes
Ingredients:
1 lb spaghetti
1 boned chicken breast
4 tbsp butter
salt and pepper
2¹/₂ oz cooked tongue
2 oz (¹/₂ cup) Gruyère cheese
1 small black truffle (optional)
1 cup heavy cream
*4 oz (1 cup) grated Parmesan
    cheese*

Cut the chicken breast into strips and sauté in a tablespoon of butter. When the chicken is golden brown, season with salt and pepper and remove from the pan. Cut the tongue, the Gruyère and the truffle into fine strips.
Boil the spaghetti in a large pot of salted water. When the pasta is almost cooked, pour a ladleful of the cooking water into a saucepan, add the cream, remaining butter and Parmesan. Heat this sauce over very low heat without letting it boil.
Preheat the oven to 400°F.
Drain the spaghetti and pour onto a hot serving dish. Pour on the sauce, mix well, season with a little freshly ground pepper and cover with the strips of chicken, tongue, Gruyère and truffle. Turn the oven off and place the dish inside the oven for a few minutes before serving.
Hint: This white sauce can also be served with egg tagliatelle. Ham may be substituted for the tongue.

Spaghetti "buried in sand"

Time: 20 minutes
Ingredients:
1 lb spaghetti
salt and pepper
¹/₄ cup olive oil
4 tbsp bread crumbs
1 tbsp chopped parsley
1 red chili pepper, chopped
2 cloves garlic, chopped

Boil the spaghetti in a large pot of salted water for about 10 minutes.
Meanwhile, pour the oil into a saucepan and heat. Add the bread crumbs, chili pepper parsley, and garlic. Season to taste.
Drain the spaghetti, pour into a serving dish and pour on the sauce. Mix well and serve.
Hint: You can complete this dish with a small handful of grated Parmesan cheese if you wish.

spaghetti "buried in sand"

Laganelle with walnut and pine nut sauce

Time: 30 minutes
Ingredients:
1 lb laganelle (thin dried
pasta noodles)
3 tbsp pine nuts
²⁄₃ cup olive oil
1¹⁄₄ cup shelled walnuts
a bunch of fresh parsley,
chopped
1 clove garlic, chopped
salt

Lightly toast the pine nuts in a frying pan with a very small amount of oil. Mix the walnuts and pine nuts and pound them with a pestle in a mortar, or chop them very fine.

Heat 2 tablespoons of the oil in a saucepan and add the chopped parsley and garlic. Sauté for a minute or two and then add the nut mixture. Allow to blend for a minute. Season with salt, remove from the heat and add a few more tablespoons of oil, stirring well.

Boil the laganelle in a large pot of salted water, drain when the pasta is *al dente* and serve with the sauce, adding 3 tablespoons of the water the pasta was cooked in to make it creamier.

Hint: This sauce can also be eaten with potato gnocchi (dumplings) or with lasagna noodles.

"Mimosa" linguine

Time: 20 minutes
Ingredients:
1 lb linguine
4 oz ham
1 cup heavy cream
2¹⁄₂ oz (²⁄₃ cup) grated Parmesan
cheese
1 tsp curry powder
¹⁄₂ tsp saffron
2 egg yolks, beaten
salt

Chop the ham and heat gently in a saucepan with the cream and cheese.

Meanwhile, boil the linguine in a large pot of salted water. Dissolve the curry powder and the saffron in a little of the water the pasta is cooking in, and add to the cream sauce. Mix well, bring to a boil and remove the saucepan from the heat. Add the beaten egg yolks and stir.

Drain the pasta when it is *al dente*, pour on the sauce and serve in a warmed dish.

Hint: Eggs are always added at the last minute, when the pan has been removed from the heat.

laganelle with walnut and pine nut sauce

Macaroni with Gruyère

Time: 20 minutes
Ingredients:
1 lb macaroni
salt and pepper
*4 oz (1 cup) shredded Gruyère
   cheese*
2 tbsp grated Parmesan cheese
4 tbsp butter

Boil the macaroni in a large pot of salted water. When the pasta is almost cooked, melt the Gruyère in about ³/₄ cup of the water the pasta is cooking in, together with the Parmesan and butter. Mix well and sprinkle with pepper. Drain the macaroni and serve with the sauce.
Hint: If you have Fontina or Swiss cheese, you may substitute them for Gruyère.

Macaroni with ricotta

Time: 20 minutes
Ingredients:
1 lb ribbed macaroni
salt
*8 oz (1 cup) ricotta, forced
   through a sieve
   a large pinch of nutmeg*
1 tsp sugar
*2 tbsp butter, cut into
   small pieces*

Boil the macaroni in a large pot of salted water. Meanwhile, mix the ricotta with a couple of tablespoons of cooking water from the pasta; add the nutmeg or cinnamon and sugar and stir well. Drain the pasta when it is *al dente*, mix in the butter and serve with the ricotta sauce.
Hint: Those on a diet may leave out the butter; the pasta will be just as appetizing.

Farmhouse-style penne

Time: 45 minutes
Ingredients:
1 lb penne
4 tbsp butter
1 small onion, finely chopped
10 oz fresh shelled peas
salt and pepper
*4 oz lean ham, cut into very
   thin strips*
¹/₂ chicken bouillon cube
*2¹/₂ oz Gruyère cheese, cut into
   small cubes*
*1 oz (¹/₄ cup) grated Parmesan
   cheese*

Heat half the butter in a large saucepan and sauté the onion. Add the peas, salt, pepper and a little water. Simmer gently. In a separate pan, brown the ham in the remaining butter and add to

farmhouse-style penne

the peas when they are almost cooked. Dissolve the bouillon cube in 1 or 2 tablespoons of water and add to the sauce. Simmer for a few more minutes.

Boil the pasta in a large pot of salted water and drain when it is *al dente*. Pour into the saucepan containing the sauce and turn up the heat for a few seconds, stirring with a wooden spoon. Complete the seasoning with the Gruyère and Parmesan cheese.

Hint: You can also add a few tablespoons of cream to the sauce, which will bind it as well as enhancing the flavor.

Maltagliati with sausage

Time: 30 minutes
Ingredients:
1 lb maltagliati
  (diamond-shaped pasta)
5 oz kielbasa-type garlic sausage
2 tbsp butter
3 to 4 tbsp olive oil
a spring of fresh rosemary or
  ¹/₄ tsp crushed dried rosemary
3 tbsp dry white wine
1 whole egg and 1 yolk
salt and pepper
2 oz (¹/₂ cup) grated Parmesan
  cheese

Cut the sausage into thin strips and brown in the butter and oil in a saucepan. Put in the rosemary to flavor. When the sausage starts to brown, sprinkle with wine and allow to evaporate.

Put the egg and the egg yolk in a large bowl and beat with a few pinches of salt, pepper and the grated cheese. Whisk well to bind the ingredients together.

Boil the pasta in a large pot of salted water and drain when the maltagliati are *al dente*. Pour the pasta into the dish containing the egg mixture and stir quickly to "cook" the egg mixture with the hot pasta. Then add the sausage and the pan juices. Mix again and serve at once.

Hint: To complete the meal, serve a main course of steak and a mixed salad of fennel, chicory, carrot and celery with a vinaigrette dressing.

Penne with frankfurters

Time: 30 minutes
Ingredients:
1 lb ribbed penne
salt
1 cup heavy cream
2 tsp wild mushroom paste
  (available at gourmet shops)
4 frankfurters, sliced

maltagliati with sausage

*2 tbsp butter cut into small
pieces*
*2 oz (½ cup) grated Parmesan
cheese*

Boil the penne in a large pot of salted water. Meanwhile, pour the cream into a saucepan and heat gently. Dissolve the mushroom paste in the cream and add the sliced frankfurters. Drain the pasta and pour into a serving dish. Mix in the butter and pour on the sauce, sprinkle with the Parmesan and stir again.
Hint: It is better to dip the frankfurters in boiling water for a few seconds to remove their skins before slicing them.

Rigatoni with pumpkin

Time: 1 ¼ hour
Ingredients:
*1 lb rigatoni or large ziti
(large fluted or smooth
dried pasta tubes)*
*2 lb pumpkin or butternut
squash*
5 tbsp butter
salt
*a few pinches of nutmeg,
preferably freshly grated*
*2 oz (½ cup) grated Parmesan
cheese*

Peel and dice the pumpkin. Melt 4 tbsp of the butter and add the diced pumpkin, simmering gently over low heat and stirring frequently.
Boil the rigatoni (or the ziti cut into 3-inches lengths), in a large pot of salted water. Drain when the pasta is *al dente* and cut the remaining butter into slivers to mix in with the pasta. Add the pumpkin and its cooking juices, some nutmeg and the cheese and mix again. Serve at once.
Hint: Reserve a few tablespoons of water from cooking the pasta and add it to the pasta just before mixing in the sauce (or add a few tablespoons of hot cream).

Rigatoni "in the pink"

Time: 45 minutes
Ingredients:
*1 lb rigatoni (large
ribbed dried pasta tubes)*
½ onion, sliced
2 tbsp butter
2 tbsp olive oil
2 oz lean bacon, diced
8 oz peeled tomatoes
salt
¼ tsp sugar
⅔ cup heavy cream

Fry the onion in the butter and

rigatoni with pumpkin

oil until it softens but does not brown. Then add the bacon and brown well before adding the tomatoes. Simmer for about 20 minutes, stirring frequently.

Add a little salt and sugar to bring out the flavor of the tomatoes. Finally, add the cream and stir until the sauce has a creamy texture.

Preheat the oven to 350°F.

Boil the rigatoni in a large pot of salted water and drain when the pasta is *al dente*. Pour into a baking dish and add the sauce. Bake in the oven for about 10 minutes.

Hint: As a main course, or as a one-course meal accompanied by the rigatoni, serve veal scaloppine lightly floured and salted, fried in butter and oil and sprinkled with a little dry Marsala.

Spicy farfalloni with walnuts

Time: 20 minutes
Ingredients:
1 lb farfalloni (large dried pasta butterflies)
salt
4 tbsp butter
10 whole walnuts, coarsely chopped

4 oz ham, diced
1 tsp white peppercorns, crushed in a mortar

Boil the farfalloni in a large pot of salted water and drain when the pasta is *al dente*. Set aside a ladleful of the water the pasta was cooked in.

In a small pan, melt the butter in the pasta water and add the walnuts, ham and pepper. Season the pasta with the sauce and serve.

Hint: A little grated Parmesan may be added to the sauce.

Conchiglie with creamy cheese sauce

Time: 25 minutes
Ingredients:
1 lb conchiglie
salt
4 oz Gorgonzola cheese, cut into small pieces
4 oz Crescenza cheese, cut into small pieces
4 to 5 tbsp milk
5 tbsp butter, cut into slivers
2 oz (1/2 cup) grated Parmesan cheese

Boil the conchiglie in a large pot of salted water.

Melt the Gorgonzola and the

Crescenza by heating them very gently in a saucepan with the milk. Stir constantly with a wooden spoon.

Warm a serving dish by pouring boiling water into it and then drying it. Drain the pasta when it is *al dente* and pour into the dish.

Mix in the butter at once and, as soon as it has melted, pour on the sauce. Sprinkle with the Parmesan cheese and serve immediately.

Hint: If you wish, you can add some freshly ground white pepper at the last minute.

Truffled sedanini

Time: 30 minutes
Ingredients:
*1 lb sedanini (small
ribbed curved macaroni)*
salt and white pepper
4 tbsp butter, cut into slivers
2 tbsp heavy cream
*4 oz (1 cup) grated Parmesan
cheese*
*1 small white truffle (optional),
cut into very thin slices*

Boil the sedanini in a large pot of salted water. Drain when the pasta is barely *al dente* and rinse under cold water briefly to stop

the cooking. Preheat the oven to 400°F.

Transfer the pasta to a baking dish and mix in the butter at once. Mix the cream and the cheese together and pour over the pasta. Scatter the truffle slices over the top and sprinkle liberally with pepper. Place in the oven for about 10 minutes.

Hint: To obtain the full pungency from pepper, keep peppercorns in a pepper mill and grind them at the last minute. White pepper is usually preferable with white sauces.

Sedanini in crab sauce

Time: 45 minutes
Ingredients:
*1 lb sedanini (small ribbed
curved macaroni)*
*¹/₂ cup crab meat, fresh or
canned*
a little dry white wine
1 bay leaf
1 carrot
1 stalk celery
1 cup heavy cream
4 tbsp butter
a pinch of paprika
salt

Simmer crab meat for 5 minutes in a *court-bouillon* of water, dry white wine, bay leaf, carrot and celery.

Drain and allow to cool. Cut half of the meat into small pieces and purée the other half with a little of the cream in a blender or food processor.

Melt three tablespoons of the butter in a saucepan and add the puréed crab, the rest of the cream and the paprika and leave on low heat allow the flavors to blend.

Meanwhile, boil the sedanini in a large pot of salted water, drain when the pasta is *al dente* and place in a preheated serving dish. Pour on the hot crab sauce. Dice the rest of the crab and sauté briefly in the remaining butter for a garnish.

Hint: It is sometimes difficult to find fresh crab meat, which is why you may have to resort to canned crab less flavorful.

Tagliatelle with triple butter sauce

Time: 1¼ hours
Ingredients:
1 lb fresh or dried tagliatelle
salt
10 tbsp butter cut into slivers
5 oz (1¼ cup) grated Parmesan
*   cheese*

Ten minutes before you are ready to eat, boil the tagliatelle in a large pot of salted water. Drain when the pasta is *al dente*. Heat a serving dish by pouring boiling water into it and then drying it. Pour in the pasta. Carefully mix in the butter and cheese and serve at once.

Hint: As this rich buttery dish is very high in calories it is advisable to eat only raw or cooked vegetables with little butter or oil for the other meals that day!

Superlative pappardelle

Time: 1½ hours
Ingredients:
1 lb fresh or dried pappardelle
4 artichokes
1 lemon
1 small onion, finely chopped
7 tbsp butter
salt and pepper
1 beef bouillon cube
a little stock
4 oz dark turkey meat, cut
*   into thin strips*
3 tbsp Madeira
1 cup heavy cream
2 oz (½ cup) grated Parmesan
*   cheese*
4 oz ham, cut into thin strips

Clean the artichokes and remove

tagliatelle with triple butter sauce

— 144 —

the thorns and the hard outer leaves. Slice the hearts and immediately immerse them in water and lemon juice to prevent them from turning black. Sauté the onion in 2 tbsp of the butter, add the sliced artichokes, salt and pepper and simmer over low heat. Dissolve half the bouillon cube in a little stock and add to the pan.

In a separate pan, brown the turkey meat in 1 tbsp of the butter and then pour in the Madeira. When the Madeira has evaporated, dissolve the rest of the bouillon cube in a tablespoon of boiling water and add to the turkey. Boil the pappardelle in a large pot of salted water. While the pasta is cooking, preheat the oven to 400°F. Drain the pasta when it is barely *al dente*. Melt the remaining butter in the saucepan the pasta was cooked in and return the pappardelle to the pan. Mix the cream in carefully, add pepper and continue cooking gently on top of the stove. Remove from the heat and mix in about half of the cheese. Spread the pasta in an even layer in the bottom of a baking dish, then cover with a layer of ham, a layer of pasta, then the artichokes and their sauce and another layer of pa-

sta; finish with a layer of turkey with its sauce. Sprinkle with the remaining cheese and put in the oven for a few minutes.

Hint: You can vary this dish by substituting chicken for the turkey and the Marsala for the Madeira.

Fettuccine with truffle

Time: 1¼ hours
Ingredients:
1 lb fresh or dried fettuccine
salt and white pepper
4 tbsp butter
2 oz (½ cup) grated Parmesan cheese
1 white truffle, thinly sliced

Boil the fettuccine in a large pot of lightly salted water and drain when the pasta is *al dente*. Heat a serving dish by pouring boiling water into it and then drying it thoroughly. Melt the butter in a small saucepan. Pour the pasta into the serving dish and pour on the butter and half the cheese. Add freshly ground pepper and mix carefully. Arrange the slices of truffle on top and serve with the rest of the cheese.

Hint: If you like, you can serve this dish with a hot meat sauce in a separate sauceboat.

fettuccine with truffle

STUFFED PASTA

Stuffed pasta means fresh egg pasta with meat or vegetable fillings. The shapes and stuffings vary from one region to another. In Emilia-Romagna, for example, you find the famous agnolini, cappelletti and ravioli; in Piedmont, agnolotti; and in Friuli-Venezia Giulia, calzoni, and so on. They all make substantial first courses.

Meat fillings are prepared from various ingredients — ground beef, veal, pork, sausage meat, giblets, smoked or cooked ham or mortadella — enriched with cheese and with egg to bind the ingredients together. Non-meat fillings are made with various vegetables — chard, spinach or other greens, squash or potatoes — sometimes mixed with ricotta or with other cheeses and spices.

Each type of stuffing requires a particular sauce for the combination of flavors to be appetizing. As a general rule, pasta with meat filling needs a rich meat ragù, while pasta with vegetable stuffing is best with delicate sauces made from butter, cream and various kinds of cheese.

There are also sauces based on mushrooms, nuts and herbs which are suited to various kinds of stuffed pasta.

A larger type of stuffed pasta are cannelloni — little rolls of fresh pasta stuffed with meat or vegetables.

Cannelloni can be served with tomato sauce or with meat ragù and are usually topped with béchamel sauce. While the types of pasta already mentioned come from the north of Italy, cannelloni, are also to be found in the center and south of Italy.

And finally, there is the rotolo — a sort of giant cannellone, made from egg pasta with a non-meat stuffing. It can be served with butter and cheese, or with a stew, or simply with tomatoes and basil. The recipes that follow will serve 6 as a first course or 4 as a main course.

Tasty agnolotti

Time: 2 hours
Ingredients:
For the pasta
3 ¹/₂ cups flour,
    either all-purpose
    or hard-wheat (semolina)
4 "large" eggs
4 to 7 tbsp water
salt
For the stuffing
4 oz calf's brain
2 oz spicy Italian sausage
8 oz braised beef
4 oz roast pork
10 oz spinach, cabbage
    or endive
2 tbsp butter
3 tbsp grated Parmesan cheese
salt and pepper
a little nutmeg
1 egg
For the sauce
meat stock
    (with the fat skimmed off)
5 tbsp butter
2 ¹/₂ oz (²/₃ cup) grated Parmesan
    cheese
4 tbsp meat roasting juices

First prepare the stuffing: scald the brain in boiling water for a few seconds and sauté the sausage in a frying pan over high heat. Mince together with the beef and pork. Boil the spinach and squeeze it thoroughly dry. Chop and sauté in the butter, then add to the meat mixture. Add the Parmesan and season with salt, pepper and nutmeg. Bind all the ingredients with the egg; you should obtain a soft but firm paste.

Prepare the egg pasta with the ingredients listed, as described on page 21. Make agnolotti following the instructions on page 34 and fill them with the meat mixture.

Boil the agnolotti in a pot of meat stock and drain when the pasta is *al dente*. Put into a dish and pour over alternate layers of melted butter and cheese and juices from the roast.

Hint: It is best to make agnolotti on days when you have ample time to spend in the kitchen; it takes a lot of patience to make the dough, and the meats require slow and attentive cooking.

Ravioli with melted butter

Time: 1 ³/₄ hours
Ingredients:
For the pasta
3 ¹/₂ cups flour,
    either all-purpose
    or hard-wheat (semolina)
6 "large" eggs
salt

tasty agnolotti

For the filling

1 small onion, chopped
2 oz smoked ham, chopped
2 tbsp butter
2 tbsp olive oil
10 oz ground veal
4 oz spicy Italian sausage
a little dry white wine
½ beef bouillon cube
salt and pepper
*1 oz (¼ cup) grated Parmesan
    cheese*
1 egg
a little nutmeg
For the sauce
5 tbsp butter
*4 fresh sage leaves or
    ¼ tsp dried sage*
*2½ oz (¼ cup) grated Parmesan
    cheese*

Sauté the onion and ham in the butter and oil. Add the veal and sausage and brown. Pour on the wine and let it evaporate. Dissolve the beef bouillon cube in a little boiling water and add to the other ingredients. Season with salt and pepper and simmer until a dry mixture is obtained. Remove from the heat and stir in the Parmesan and the egg. Season with nutmeg.

Prepare the egg pasta with the ingredients listed, following the instructions on page 21.

Make ravioli as described on page 36, and fill with the stuffing. Boil the ravioli in a large pot of salted water, drain and place in a dish. Heat the butter with the sage until the butter is hazelnut colored. Pour it over the ravioli, alternating with the cheese.

Hint: Leftover braised or roast meat can be added to the stuffing if you wish.

Ravioli stuffed with spinach and ricotta

Time: 1½ hours
Ingredients:
For the pasta
*3½ cups flour,
    either all-purpose
    or hard-wheat (semolina)*
6 "large" eggs
salt
For the filling
2¼ lb spinach or greens
salt
1 tbsp chopped parsley
*2½ oz (⅔ cup) grated Parmesan
    cheese*
8 oz (1 cup) ricotta
1 egg
a little nutmeg
For the sauce
7 tbsp butter
salt
*2½ oz (⅔ cup) grated Parmesan
    cheese*

ravioli stuffed with spinach and ricotta

Remove the stems and wash the spinach thoroughly. Cook until wilted in a frying pan without adding any more water (the water remaining on the leaves will be sufficient). Add salt and simmer in the uncovered pan. Drain and squeeze dry in a clean towel. Let cool, then chop and put into a bowl. Add the parsley, Parmesan, ricotta, egg and nutmeg and mix.

Prepare the egg pasta following the instructions on page 21 and make ravioli as described on page 36. Fill with the stuffing. Boil the ravioli uncovered, in a large pot of salted water over medium heat. Meanwhile, melt the butter with a pinch of salt.

As the ravioli gradually float to the surface, drain them with a slotted spoon and season them with the melted butter and Parmesan in alternate layers.

Hint: To prevent the dough from drying out, roll it out two or three times before filling it. Do not drain the ravioli in a colander as with other types of pasta; the ravioli may stick and break, and the filling will be lost.

Cappelletti with mushroom sauce

Time: 1³/₄ hours

Ingredients:

For the pasta

3¹/₂ cups flour,
  either all-purpose or
  hard-wheat (semolina)

6 "large" eggs

salt

For the filling

2 tbsp butter

1 tbsp olive oil

8 oz turkey or chicken meat,
  cut into fine strips

2 oz smoked ham, cut into fine
  strips

1 slice of mortadella, cut into
  fine strips

salt and pepper

2 fresh or dried sage leaves

2 chicken livers

2 tbsp Marsala

4 oz (1 cup) grated Parmesan
  cheese

2 tbsp bread crumbs

1 egg

a little nutmeg

For the sauce

1 oz dried mushrooms

4 tbps butter

1 clove garlic

a little dry white wine

salt and pepper

¹/₄ beef bouillon cube, crumbled

1 cup heavy cream

a bunch of fresh parsley,
  chopped

1 oz (¹/₄ cup) grated Parmesan
  cheese

cappelletti with mushroom sauce

First prepare the filling: melt the butter with 1 tablespoon of oil and add the meat, the ham and the mortadella or bologna. Season with salt and pepper and add the sage. Brown and then add the chicken livers. Pour on 2 tablespoons of Marsala and allow to evaporate.

Remove the pan from the heat and take out the sage leaves. Chop the mixture, preferably in a meat grinder, and collect it in a bowl. Add the ricotta, the Parmesan, the bread crumbs, the egg and some grated nutmeg and mix well to obtain a smooth paste. Taste and add salt if necessary.

Prepare the egg pasta with the ingredients listed, following the instructions on page 21. Make cappelletti as described on page 34 and stuff with the filling.

While they are drying, prepare the sauce: soften the mushrooms in warm water, slice them and brown them in the butter with the whole clove of garlic. Pour in the wine and allow it to evaporate. Add salt, pepper and the beef bouillon cube and simmer for a few minutes. Add the cream, bring to a boil and sprinkle with parsley just before removing the pan from the heat. Boil the cappelletti in a large pot of salted water. Drain and pour on alternate layers of mushroom sauce and Parmesan, or finish the pasta with butter and serve the sauce separately.

Hint: Use fresh cèpes-wood when in season. Do not wash them: it is sufficient to cut off the bottom of the stems and wipe the top with a damp cloth.

Cappelletti pie

Time: 3 hours
Ingredients:
1 lb fresh cappelletti
salt
1 tbsp butter
a few tbsp bread crumbs
2¹/₂ oz (²/₃ cup) grated Parmesan
   cheese
1 egg
For the pastry
2 cups all-purpose flour
salt
7 tbsp butter
2 tbsp sugar
3 egg yolks
For the ragù
5 tbsp butter
2 oz bacon, chopped
1 onion, chopped
1 carrot, chopped
1 stalk celery, chopped
5 oz pork loin, ground
5 oz lean ground beef

1 lb ripe tomatoes, peeled
*   and forced through a sieve*
*   or one 18-oz can*
*   peeled tomatoes*
1 clove
1 bay leaf
salt and pepper
⅓ cup heavy cream
2 to 3 chicken livers, finely
*   diced*

For the béchamel
3 tbsp butter
2 tbsp flour
2 cups milk, heated
salt and pepper
a little nutmeg

First, prepare the ragù: heat half of the butter and sauté the bacon, onion, carrot and celery. Add the ground meats and brown. Add the tomato, clove, bay leaf, a pinch of salt and pepper and simmer for about 1 hour, adding a little cream from time to time. Add the chicken livers a few minutes before the sauce is cooked.

While the ragù is simmering, prepare the sweet pastry: pour the flour onto a pastry board in a heap and make a well in the center. Put in a pinch of salt, the butter, the sugar and 3 egg yolks. Mix vigorously to incorporate the flour into the eggs and butter. When you have a smooth dough (knead it as little as possible with your hands), place it in plastic wrap and put it in the lowest part of the refrigerator.

Meanwhile, make a béchamel sauce with 3 tablespoons of the butter, 2 tablepoons of flour and the milk. Season with salt, pepper and nutmeg. Bring to a boil and remove from the heat.

Boil the cappelletti in a large pot of salted water, drain when the pasta is *al dente* and pour on some of the ragù. Divide the pastry into two pieces, one twice the size of the other. Roll out the larger piece into a round ⅛ inch thick. Butter a 10-inch deep pie dish and sprinkle with bread crumbs. Line the dish with the larger piece of dough. Pour in the cappelletti, alternating them with ragù, béchamel and grated Parmesan. Cover with the other piece of pastry cut into a round the same diameter as the pie dish. Cut off any extra pastry and seal the pie with the prongs of a fork all around the edge. Make a small hole in the center and insert a small funnel made of aluminum foil to enable the steam to escape during cooking. Then beat the whole egg and brush the pastry with it.

Place the pie in the oven (preheated to 350°F) for about 1

hour. Remove from the oven and let rest for a few minutes before serving.

Hint: If you do not like the combination of sweet and savory, you can omit the sugar from the pastry. You can, of course, substitute ready-made frozen pie crust dough.

Pumpkin tortelli

Time: 2$\frac{1}{2}$ hours
Ingredients:
For the pasta
3$\frac{1}{2}$ cups flour,
*   either all-purpose or*
*   hard-wheat (semolina)*
6 "large" eggs
salt
For the filling and the sauce
4$\frac{1}{2}$ lb pumpkin or butternut
*   squash*
3 oz (³/₄ cup) ground almonds
4 oz (1 cup) grated Parmesan
*   cheese*
1 lemon
1 oz candied citron peel,
*   finely chopped*
a little nutmeg
1 egg
salt and pepper
bread crumbs (optional)
2 tbsp butter
2 tbsp olive oil
6 fresh or dried sage leaves

First, prepare the filling: slice the pumpkin or squash and remove the seeds, then bake in the oven. Scoop out the soft flesh with a large spoon and throw away the peel.

Force the pumpkin or squash through a sieve and add the ground almonds, half the Parmesan, the grated lemon rind (grate only the yellow surface, not the white pith), the candied peel, nutmeg, the egg and a pinch of salt and pepper. Mix thoroughly with a wooden spoon. If the mixture is too soft, add a small quantity of bread crumbs.

Make the egg pasta with the ingredients listed, following the instructions on page 21. Make half-moon-shaped tortelli and fill them with the pumpkin or squash stuffing.

Boil the tortelli in a large pot of salted water until *al dente*. Meanwhile, heat the butter and oil with the sage. Drain the tortelli into a serving dish, pouring on alternate layers of the butter sauce (discard the sage) and the rest of the Parmesan.

Hint: To give the tortelli a pleasing shape, cut them out with a serrated pastry cutter, making the circles about two inches in diameter.

Brescia-style casonsei

Time: 1 ½ hours
Ingredients:
For the pasta
3 ½ cups flour,
   either all-purpose
   or hard-wheat (semolina)
6 "large" eggs
salt
For the stuffing
1 slice bread, crust discarded
a little milk
10 oz sausage meat,
   crumbled into small pieces
4 oz (1 cup) grated Parmesan
   cheese
salt and pepper
For the sauce
7 tbsp butter
a few fresh or dried sage leaves
pepper
4 oz (1 cup) grated Parmesan
   cheese

First prepare the filling: soak the bread in a little milk. Squeeze it out by hand and put into a bowl with the sausage meat, cheese and salt and pepper if you wish. Mix well.

Prepare the egg pasta with the ingredients listed, following the instructions on page 21. Make large ravioli in the shape of calzoncini (half-moon shapes), as described on page 36, and fill with the stuffing.

Boil the casonsei in a large pot of salted water. While the pasta is cooking, melt the butter with the sage and a pinch of pepper. Drain the casonsei with a slotted spoon and serve with the sage-flavored butter and Parmesan.

Hint: Wait a few minutes before serving the casonsei to allow the pasta to fully absorb the flavor of the sauce, and the cheese to melt.

Casonsei with pumpkin and pheasant

Time: 2 ½ hours
Ingredients:
For the pasta
3 ½ cups flour,
   either all-purpose or
   hard-wheat (semolina)
6 "large" eggs
salt
For the filling
1 ½ lb pumpkin, seeded
   and peeled
2 oz (½ cup) grated Parmesan
   cheese
8 oz (1 cup) ricotta
salt and pepper
1 egg
For the sauce and to season the casonsei
1 pheasant weighing

about 1 1/4 lb, dressed
4 oz sliced bacon
salt
peppercorns
a few fresh or dried sage leaves
2 tbsp butter
a few tbsp olive oil
1 oz (1/4 cup) grated Parmesan
   cheese

First, prepare the filling for the casonsei: bake the pumpkin (or, if you don't have the time, boil it) and force it through a sieve. Collect the purée in a bowl and add the Parmesan, the ricotta, salt, pepper and the egg. Mix well.

Prepare the egg pasta with the ingredients listed, following the instructions on page 21. Make large calzoncini as described on page 36. Fill them with the pumpkin mixture.

Preheat the oven to 425°F.

Chop the pheasant's liver and gizzards (if you have them) together with half the bacon, salt, a few peppercorns and the sage. Stuff the pheasant with the mixture and truss the bird. Butter a baking dish and sprinkle with oil. Place the bird in the dish and cover with the remaining bacon. Roast in the oven for about 1 hour. When it is cooked, remove all the meat and cut it into tiny pieces. Scoop out the stuffing.

Skim the fat off the juices which will have collected in the dish the bird was cooked in and add the crumbled stuffing and the pheasant meat; heat for 1 minute.

Ten minutes before you are ready to serve, boil the casonsei in a large pot of salted water. Drain, a few at a time, with a slotted spoon, and arrange in a serving dish.

Alternate with layers of the pheasant sauce. To complete, sprinkle the grated Parmesan over the top.

Hint: This typical dish from Lombardy can be served as a main course.

Marubini with financière sauce

Time: 1 1/2 hours
Ingredients:
For the pasta
3 1/2 cups flour,
   either all-purpose
   or hard-wheat (semolina)
6 "large" eggs
salt
For the filling
8 oz braised or roast beef,
   chopped

4 oz roast veal, chopped
*4 oz boiled calf's brain,
    chopped*
*2¹/₂ oz (²/₃ cup) grated Parmesan
    cheese*
salt and pepper
a little nutmeg
1 to 2 eggs
For the ragù
3 tbsp butter
¹/₂ carrot, chopped,
¹/₂ onion, chopped
¹/₂ stalk celery, chopped
3 chicken gizzards and
*4 chicken livers, cleaned
    and coarsely chopped*
*1 oz dried mushrooms, soaked,
    drained and sliced*
¹/₄ cup dry white wine
a little stock, heated
salt
1 tsp flour

First prepare the filling: mix the chopped beef, veal and brain in a bowl and add the Parmesan, salt, pepper, nutmeg and an egg to bind the ingredients together. You may find you need 2 eggs. You should obtain a soft but dry mixture.

Now prepare the ragù: melt the butter in a pan over a moderate heat and sauté the carrot, onion and celery. Add the gizzards and, when they are almost cooked, the livers and mushrooms.

Brown for a few minutes, then pour the wine over the giblets. When the wine has evaporated, pour in a little hot stock. Add salt, cover and simmer for about 30 minutes. When cooked, add a tablespoon of butter mixed with the flour to thicken the ragù.

Prepare the egg pasta with the ingredients listed, following the instructions on page 21. Make marubini as described on page 38 and stuff with the filling.

Boil the marubini in a large pot of salted water or stock, drain and serve with the ragù.

Hint: If the stuffing mixture is too firm, add more egg, or, if it is too moist, add bread crumbs. The traditional regional recipe suggests cooking the marubini in a good meat stock, but they are just as tasty boiled in water and drained — in which case, they can be made a little bigger.

Trieste-style ofelle

Time: 2 hours
Ingredients:
For the pasta
2¹/₄ lb baking potatoes
salt
1¹/₂ cups all-purpose flour
1 egg
1 tsp dry yeast

For the filling
2 lb spinach or other greens
4 oz pure pork sausage,
  chopped
5 oz ground veal
salt
2 tbsp butter
1 onion, chopped
1 tbsp chopped parsley
1 clove garlic, chopped
For the sauce
7 tbsp sweet butter
4 oz (1 cup) grated Parmesan
  cheese

First prepare the filling: wash the spinach (or other greens), drain, boil in a little water, drain well, chop and put into a bowl with the sausage, veal and salt. Heat the butter and sauté the onion, then add the contents of the bowl. Simmer over a low heat for a few minutes. Add the parsley and garlic, sauté briefly and remove from the heat. Let cool.

Now make the pasta: boil the potatoes in salted water, peel and mash them. Put the mashed potatoes on the pastry board, add the flour, egg, salt and yeast and mix to a dough similar to that for potato gnocchi but a bit firmer.

Roll out the pastry and make large ravioli (see page 36) and stuff with the filling. Boil in a large pot of salted water, drain and serve with melted butter and Parmesan.

Hint: The dough will seem rather moist because it is prepared with potatoes. Use a long spatula to ease it off the pastry board from time to time.

Panciuti "al preboggion"

Time: 2 hours
Ingredients:
For the pasta
3 1/2 cups flour,
  either all-purpose
  or hard-wheat (semolina)
1 to 1 1/4 cups dry white wine
salt
For the filling
3 lb mixed greens (chard,
  cabbage leaves, fresh grape
  leaves, spinach, dandelion, etc.)
a bunch of chopped parsley
1 clove garlic, finely chopped
2 eggs
2 1/2 oz (2/3 cup) grated Parmesan
  cheese
5 oz (2/3 cup) ricotta
salt and pepper
For the sauce
5 oz (1 1/4 cups) walnuts
2 slices soft bread, crust
  discarded, soaked in water
  and thoroughly squeezed out

panciuti "al preboggion"

3 tbsp pine nuts (optional)
salt
1 clove garlic
¹/₃ to ¹/₂ cup heavy cream
3 to 4 tbsp olive oil

First prepare the filling: wash the greens and boil in a little water. Drain well, chop finely and put in a bowl. Add the parsley, garlic, eggs, Parmesan, ricotta, salt and pepper and mix. Prepare the pasta with the ingredients listed, following the instructions on page 21. Cut the dough into large rounds (or triangles if you prefer) and make triangular or half-moon-shaped ravioli as described on page 36. Stuff with the filling.

Before cooking the panciuti, prepare the sauce: put the walnuts, bread, pine nuts, a few pinches of salt and the garlic into a mortar, blender or food processor, and blend to a paste. Force this paste through a sieve and dilute with the cream to obtain a thickish sauce. Stir in the olive oil.

Boil the panciuti in a large pot of salted water, drain and serve with the walnut sauce.

Hint: "Preboggion" is a mixture of herbs which grow wild in the Ligurian hills where this dish originated.

To make a close approximation of "preboggion", use up to a half pound of borage and four ounces fresh chervil as part of the greens and omit the chopped parsley.

Pasta piena with cheese sauce

Time: 1¹/₂ hours
Ingredients:
For the pasta
3¹/₂ cups flour,
either all-purpose
or hard-wheat (semolina)
6 "large" eggs
salt
For the filling
8 oz beef marrow
4 oz ham, finely chopped
3 oz (³/₄ cup) grated Parmesan cheese
4 eggs
salt and pepper
a little nutmeg
a few tbsp bread crumbs
For the sauce
7 tbsp butter
1 cup heavy cream
salt and pepper
4 oz (1 cup) shredded Gruyère cheese

First prepare the filling: blanch the beef marrow in boiling water and force it through a sieve into a bowl with the ham, Parmesan, the eggs, a pinch of pepper, salt, nutmeg and bread crumbs (enough to obtain a fairly soft mixture). Mix with a wooden spoon to obtain a smooth paste. Prepare the egg pasta with the ingredients listed, following the instructions on page 21. Shape the pasta as described on page 40 and stuff with the filling.

Boil the filled pasta in a large pot of salted water or stock until *al dente*. Meanwhile, prepare the sauce: melt the butter in a large pan, add the cream and allow it to reduce and thicken a little. Add salt and pepper and the Gruyère. Stir over a low heat until the cheese has melted.

Drain the pasta and pour into the pan with the sauce. Stir carefully for a few seconds and serve while the sauce is still 'gooey'.

Hint: You can add Gorgonzola cheese to the sauce if you prefer a more hot flavor. According to the regional recipe, the pasta is cooked in stock, but it is also excellent when boiled in water.

Cannelloni with mascarpone

Time: 1½ hours
Ingredients:
1 lb homemade or packaged
lasagna noodles
1 lb spinach, or other
greens
8 oz (1 cup) ricotta
3 oz mascarpone cheese
salt and pepper
4 tbsp butter
2 tbsp flour
1 cup milk
⅓ cup heavy cream
5 oz Fontina cheese,
half grated, half cubed

Boil the greens, chop and mix them with the ricotta, mascarpone, salt and pepper.

Melt 2 tablespoons of the butter and incorporate the flour. Boil the milk and add it gradually, stirring continuously. Simmer for a few minutes and stir in the cream. Bring to a boil, stirring constantly, add the grated Fontina and remove from the heat.

Preheat the oven to 350°F.

Boil the lasagna noodles in a large pot of salted water, drain when the pasta is *al dente* and lay it on a clean towel. Put a little of the cheese and vegetable mixture in the center of each rectangle, roll the noodles up and arrange the cannelloni in a large buttered baking dish. Cover with the sauce. Scatter over the cubes of Fontina and top with slivers of butter. Bake in the oven for about 15 minutes.

Hint: To make a lighter dish, omit the mascarpone and increase the amount of ricotta, which must be very fresh and soft.

Cannelloni filled with chicken

Time: 1³/₄ hours
Ingredients:
1 lb homemade lasagna noodles
For the filling
2 tbsp olive oil
1¹/₂ tbsp butter
2 lb frying chicken parts
salt and pepper
1 lemon, squeezed
4 oz smoked ham
*2 oz (¹/₂ cup) grated Parmesan
    cheese*
2 eggs
For the sauce
2 tbsp olive oil
4 tbsp butter
1 small onion, chopped
*one 8-oz can peeled tomatoes,
    forced through a sieve*
salt
*2 oz (¹/₂ cup) grated Parmesan
    cheese*

First prepare the filling: heat the oil and the butter and brown the chicken. Add salt and pepper and the juice from the lemon. Cook the chicken, turning it often. Drain, discard the skin, remove all the meat and put it through a meat grinder with the ham. Mix in the Parmesan cheese, eggs, salt and some of the juices from the pan in which the chicken was cooked. Now make the tomato sauce: heat the oil and 1¹/₂ tablespoons of the butter and soften the onion, then add the tomato and salt. Simmer until the sauce thickens. Preheat the oven to 350°F. Boil the lasagna noodles, a few at a time, in a large pot of salted water, drain when the pasta is *al dente* and lay the lasagna on a clean towel. Place a little filling in the center of each rectangle and roll up to make cannelloni. Arrange them in layers in a buttered baking dish, pouring a little tomato sauce over each layer. Sprinkle the cheese and the remaining butter over the top. Place in the oven for 15 minutes.

Hint: This light, chicken-based filling is particularly recommended for children. The dish is also delicious served with a sauce made with fresh mushrooms.

Three-colored cannelloni

Time: 1³/₄ hours

Ingredients:
1 lb homemade lasagna noodles
4 oz cooked chicken meat
2¹/₂ oz ham
2 tbsp butter
3 tbsp flour
1¹/₂ cups milk
salt
a little nutmeg
4 oz (1 cup) shredded Gruyère
  cheese
For the sauce
4 tbsp butter
2 tbsp olive oil
¹/₂ onion, chopped
1¹/₄ lb ripe tomatoes
10 to 12 oz fresh young peas
salt
grated Parmesan cheese

First prepare the filling: chop the chicken meat with the ham. In a saucepan, melt the butter and incorporate the flour. Boil the milk and add it gradually to the flour and butter. Season with salt and nutmeg and stir in the Gruyère, chicken and ham.

Now prepare the sauce: heat half the butter and the oil and sauté the onion. Add the tomato, the peas and salt. Simmer until the peas are cooked and the sauce has thickened.

Preheat the oven to 350°F.

Boil the lasagna noodles, a few at a time, in a large pot of salted water, drain when the pasta is *al dente* and lay on a clean towel to dry. Place a little filling in the center of each rectangle and roll up to make cannelloni. Sprinkle a little of the sauce in the bottom of a baking dish and arrange half the cannelloni in it. Cover with some of the sauce and a little Parmesan, then make another layer of cannelloni and cover with the rest of the sauce and more Parmesan. Sprinkle a few slivers of butter and Parmesan over the top and place in the oven for about 15 minutes.

Hint: You can use leftover chicken or turkey for this filling.

Stuffed shells

Time: 1 hour
Ingredients:
1 lb large ribbed pasta shells
for stuffing
1 small onion, chopped
4 tbsp butter
10 oz ground beef
4 oz sausage meat, crumbled
1 tsp flour
1 tsp tomato paste
a little nutmeg
preferably freshly grated
a small bunch of fresh parsley
chopped, a little stock
salt

1 cup fairly thin béchamel sauce
2 oz grated Parmesan cheese

Sauté the onion in 1 to 2 tablespoons of the butter and add the beef and sausage. When the meat has browned, incorporate the flour and mix. Add the tomato paste, the nutmeg and the parsley. Continue simmering, gradually adding a little stock for about 30 minutes.

Preheat the oven to 400°F. Boil the pasta in a large pot of salted water, and drain when the pasta is *al dente*. Cover the table with a towel and pour the shells out onto the cloth to dry. Stuff with the meat filling using a pastry bag fitted with a smooth, wide tip or use a spoon.

Butter a baking dish and arrange the shell in one or two layers. Cover with the béchamel sauce. Sprinkle on the cheese and a few slivers of butter and bake until the surface is golden brown.

Hint: To make the béchamel sauce, use only one tablespoon each butter and flour, 1 cup milk, and ¼ teaspoon salt.

Stuffed pasta roll with melted butter

Time: 2 hours

Ingredients:
For the pasta
1 ³⁄₄ cups flour, either all-purpose or hard-wheat
3 "large" eggs
salt
For the filling
2 lb fresh spinach
2 tbsp butter
8 oz (1 cup) ricotta
1 oz (¼ cup) grated Parmesan cheese
salt and pepper
For the sauce
5 tbsp butter
a few fresh or dried sage leaves
2 oz (½ cup) grated Parmesan cheese

First prepare the filling: wash and boil the spinach or other greens. Squeeze out thoroughly, chop and mix in the butter. Let cool. Mash the ricotta with a fork, then mix with the spinach, the Parmesan, salt and pepper.

Prepare the egg pasta with the ingredients listed on page 21. Form into a roll and stuff with the filling. Serve it in slices with the melted butter, sage and Parmesan.

Hint: If some of the roll is left over, arrange the slices in a baking dish and cover with a very thin béchamel sauce. Heat through in the oven.

stuffed pasta roll with melted butter

GNOCCHI

Gnocchi are a popular Italian specialty which vary in
appearance and accompanying sauces from one region to
another. There are many different types of gnocchi and they
are all good whether made with potatoes, spinach,
pumpkin, carrot, cereal grains or bread and cheese.
The most commonly found variety in Italian kitchens are
the gnocchi made from starchy vegetables and flour, or
flour alone. They are boiled or baked in the oven, and
often flavored with eggs, cheese or greens. The dough is
usually prepared on a pastry board unless, like ricotta
gnocchi, it is mixed in a bowl. For the famous Choux Paste
Gnocchi or *gnocchi alla parigina*, the dough is cooked in a
saucepan directly over the heat.
Most types of gnocchi require kneading quickly and lightly,
allowing the dough to retain its characteristic puffiness; if
you touch it too much and heat it with your hands, it is
likely to become moisty and sticky. For potato gnocchi, use
a potato masher rather than a food mill to obtain a purée
that will not be sticky. For semolina gnocchi, you need a
marble or non-absorbent slab on which to leave the dough
to cool before shaping it. For gnocchi made from choux
paste, use a round-bottomed, long-handled saucepan.
Nearly all gnocchi are cooked by boiling in a large pot of
salted water. They are removed with the help of a slotted
spoon as soon as they float to the surface and are served in
layers with a great variety of different sauces. With the more
delicate types of gnocchi, like ricotta gnocchi, it is best to
serve a sauce of melted butter and cheese, or cream, while
for potato or other vegetable gnocchi, tomato, tomato and
mushroom sauce and even meat ragù are recommended.
The recipes that follow will serve 6 as a first course or 4 as
a main course.

Potato gnocchi with tomato sauce

Time: 1¼ hours
Ingredients:
For the gnocchi
2¼ lbs baking potatoes
salt
a pinch of nutmeg
about 2 cups all-purpose flour
1 egg
For the sauce
2 tbsp olive oil
4 tbsp butter
1 small onion, chopped
1 clove garlic
1 lb ripe tomatoes (or
   one 8-oz can peeled tomatoes
   forced through a sieve
a few fresh basil leaves
salt
2½ oz (⅔ cup) grated Parmesan
   cheese

Prepare the gnocchi: wash the potatoes and put them in a pot. Cover with ample cold water, add salt and boil. Drain and peel the potatoes and, while they are still hot, mash them and heap the purée on the pastry board. Add a pinch of salt and a pinch of nutmeg. Sprinkle with flour, make a well in the center and break the egg into it; mix, adding a little more flour if necessary. You should end up with a smooth dough that no longer sticks to your hands. Do not add too much flour; it will make the gnocchi hard when cooked.

Divide the dough into pieces and roll them on the pastry board with the palms of your hands to make long sticks. Cut each stick into 1-inch lengths and flour them. Then press them against the back of a grater or on the prongs of a fork to give them the characteristic fluted appearance (or you can use the little wood block specially made for the purpose). As you make them, lay them separately on the floured pastry board.

While the potatoes are boiling, prepare the sauce: heat the oil and butter and sauté the onion with the whole clove of garlic. Add the tomato and the whole basil leaves. Season with salt and simmer over low heat until the sauce thickens.

Boil the gnocchi in two or three batches in a large pot of salted water; as soon as they begin to float on the surface, scoop them out with a slotted spoon and drain them. Serve in layers with the sauce (remove the garlic) and the Parmesan cheese.

Hint: To enrich the dish, add a few dots of butter to the gnocchi before serving.

potato gnocchi with tomato sauce

Semolina gnocchi

Time: 1 1/2 hours
Ingredients:
For the gnocchi
4 cups milk
1 3/4 cups hard-wheat flour
4 tbsp butter
salt and pepper
3 egg yolks
a little nutmeg
2 oz (1/2 cup) grated Parmesan
  cheese
For the sauce
5 tbsp butter
a few fresh or dried sage leaves
2 1/2 oz (2/3 cup) grated Parmesan
  cheese

First make the dough for the gnocchi: heat the milk, cut the butter into pieces and add to the milk together with salt and bring to a boil. Sprinkle in the semolina steadily, stirring quickly with a wooden spoon to prevent lumps forming. Continue mixing over the heat until the mixture resembles a very thick sort of polenta.

Remove from the heat when the mixture begins to come away from the sides of the pan. Add the egg yolks, one at a time, a few pinches of nutmeg, the cheese, and pepper, if you wish. Pour the mixture onto a marble slab or a smooth buttered surface, flatten it with a spatula to a thickness of about 1/2 inch and let cool and harden. Then, using a cutter, or a glass with a diameter of about 1 1/2 inches, cut the dough into rounds. Dip the cutter in boiling water from time to time. Preheat the oven to 350°F. Arrange the gnocchi in a buttered baking dish, heaping them up a little.

For the sauce, melt the butter with the sage leaves and pour over the gnocchi. Sprinkle with cheese and bake in the oven until the gnocchi are golden brown.

Hint: This dish is also good as an accompaniment to meat roasts or stews.

Spinach and ricotta gnocchi

Time: 40 minutes
Ingredients:
2 lb spinach
8 oz (1 cup) ricotta
5 oz (1 1/4 cups) grated Parmesan
  cheese
2 eggs
salt and pepper
a pinch of nutmeg
about 1 1/4 cups all-purpose flour
7 tbsp butter

Clean and wash the spinach

thoroughly. Drain and place in a pot. Cook the spinach in the water remaining on the leaves. Drain and cut into strips, then chop. Mix with the ricotta, half the Parmesan, the eggs, a pinch of salt, pepper and nutmeg and the flour to obtain a mixture that is not too moist. Flour your hands frequently and shape little balls about the size of walnuts.

Bring a large shallow pan of salted water to a boil, immerse the gnocchi a few at a time and remove them with a slotted spoon as they rise to the surface. Heat the butter until it is hazelnut-colored and pour over the gnocchi with the rest of the cheese.

Hint: To prevent the mixture from being too moist, you can dry the chopped spinach over a very low heat before mixing it with the ricotta.

Pumpkin gnocchi

Time: 1 hour 50 minutes
Ingredients:
For the gnocchi
2½ lb pumpkin
 or butternut squash
a pinch of nutmeg
1 egg
about 1²⁄₃ cups all-purpose flour
salt

For the sauce
5 tbsp butter
2½ oz (²⁄₃ cup) grated Parmesan cheese

Cut the pumpkin into pieces, peel, discard the seeds and fibers and bake in the oven or boil in salted water until tender.

Force the pumpkin through a sieve into a bowl and add the nutmeg and egg. Sift in the flour a little at a time. You should obtain a fairly thick mixture.

Bring a large pot of salted water to a boil. Place teaspoonfuls of the mixture in the water. Work quickly and use a slotted spoon to drain the gnocchi as soon as they float to the surface. Pour melted butter and cheese over the gnocchi. Serve immediately.

Hint: This type of gnocchi may also be served with a simple basil and tomato sauce.

Choux paste gnocchi

Time: 1¼ hours
Ingredients:
For the gnocchi
1 cup milk
salt
a little nutmeg
5 tbsp butter cut into pieces
³⁄₄ cup all-purpose flour

3 to 4 eggs
2 tbsp grated Parmesan cheese
For the sauce
7 tbsp butter
¹/₂ cup flour
2 cups milk, heated
salt
4 oz (1 cup) grated Parmesan
  cheese

Prepare the gnocchi dough first: pour the milk into a large saucepan with a few pinches of salt and nutmeg and the butter. Bring to a boil. Remove the saucepan from the heat for a moment and pour in the flour all at once, stirring vigorously with a wooden spoon to stop lumps forming. Replace the pan over the heat and continue stirring until the dough is dry and comes away from the sides of the saucepan. It should make a slight noise as if it were being fried. Allow to cool, stirring frequently and incorporating the eggs one at a time. If the dough is too firm, add a fourth egg. Finally, add the cheese and knead the dough for 10 minutes.

Meanwhile bring a large pan of salted water to a boil. Put the dough in a pastry bag with a wide plain tip about ¹/₂ inch in diameter. Squeeze the bag to produce a cylinder of dough about 1 inch long and drop it straight into the boiling water, using a knife to cut off the dough cleanly. Turn the heat down as low as possible. Continue until you have used up all the dough. Boil the gnocchi for 8 to 9 minutes. Drain with a slotted spoon and place on a clean towel to dry.

To make the sauce, melt 3 tablespoons of the butter in a saucepan. Add the flour and stir, then add the hot milk, a little at a time. Season with salt and let the sauce thicken. Remove from the heat and add half the cheese.

Preheat the oven to 350°F.

Arrange the gnocchi in a buttered baking dish. Melt the remaining butter and pour some over the gnocchi, then pour on about two-thirds of the béchamel sauce. Sprinkle with a little grated cheese and mix together carefully. Spread the gnocchi out and pour over the remaining sauce, melted butter and the rest of the cheese. Place in the oven for 10 minutes, then turn the oven up to 400°F and leave for a further 10 minutes.

Hint: The gnocchi can also be served with a sauce based on Gorgonzola and Mascarpone cheeses.

CRÊPES

Crêpes are made from a batter of milk, flour and eggs, which is fried paper-thin and stuffed with various fillings based on meat, on spinach and ricotta or on other vegetable mixtures. Once they are filled they can be rolled up, folded in four, or stacked one on top of the other to make a kind of layer cake. Finally, they are covered with smooth béchamel sauce and baked in the oven. Because the ingredients are so rich and filling, crêpes are usually served as a main course. To make crêpes, you need a small frying pan about 4 to 5 inches in diameter with a long handle, or a non-stick pan which makes it possible to make crêpes without additional fat.
The cooking process is simplified if you use an electric crêpe maker, equipped with a round plate onto which the runny batter is poured. A very hot hotplate is pressed down on top of it. After it has been turned over and the lid opened, the mixture on the hotplate is paper-thin and cooked. The crêpe can be removed with a spatula and laid on a plate.
To obtain very thin crêpes, the batter should be fairly runny so that it will spread easily and evenly over the bottom of the frying pan. The pan should be placed over a medium heat so that the batter will stick immediately but without burning.
It is customary to let the batter rest before making the crêpes (anywhere between half an hour and several hours). This enables the ingredients to combine and makes the batter less elastic.
Crêpes can also be stored in the freezer for several months. If you are freezing crêpes in a béchamel sauce, use very little butter; you can always add slivers of butter when you bake the crêpe in the oven.
The recipes that follow will serve 6 as a first course or 4 as a main course.

Priest's housekeeper's crêpes

Time: 1½ hours
Ingredients:
For the crêpes
4 eggs
salt
¾ cup all-purpose flour
½ cup milk
1 tbsp butter or lard
For the filling
½ small onion, chopped
1 tbsp butter
1 chicken liver, chopped
  into small pieces
4 oz sweetbreads, chopped
  into small pieces
salt
4 oz ham
10 oz spinach, boiled,
  drained and chopped
5 oz ricotta
1 egg
2 oz (½ cup) grated Parmesan
  cheese
a little nutmeg
For the sauce
4 tbsp butter
3 tbsp flour
2 cups milk, heated
salt
2 oz (½ cup) grated Parmesan
  cheese

First make the crêpes: beat the eggs in a bowl with a pinch of salt. Add the flour and mix thoroughly to obtain a smooth mixture with no lumps. Add the milk, a little at a time, stirring constantly. You should end up with a fairly runny mixture. Cover with a plate and let rest for at least 30 minutes. Melt the butter in an iron or non-stick long-handled frying pan and heat. When the pan is hot, pour in a ladleful of the crêpe batter, shaking the pan with a circular motion so that the mixture forms a thin, even layer on the bottom of the pan. As soon as the crêpe has formed, toss it and cook the other side. Remove each crêpe and keep it warm. Continue making crêpes until the batter is used up.

Now prepare the filling: fry the onion in the butter and add the chicken liver, sweetbread and salt and sauté for a few minutes. Transfer the mixture to a bowl and finely chop with the ham. Mix in the spinach, ricotta, egg, Parmesan, a little grated nutmeg and salt.

At this point, prepare the béchamel sauce: melt 3 tablespoons of the butter in a saucepan and incorporate the flour. Stir well to eliminate any lumps and pour in the hot milk a little at a time. Add salt and half the Parmesan.

Preheat the oven to 375°F.

Place some filling in the center of each crêpe and roll it up. Pour a little béchamel sauce into a baking dish and arrange the crêpes in it. Pour on the rest of the béchamel and sprinkle with Parmesan and the remaining butter cut into slivers. Bake in the oven for 10 to 15 minutes. Serve from the same dish.

Hint: To avoid the formation of lumps in the crêpe mixture, break in the eggs one at a time and incorporate a tablespoon of flour between each egg until all the eggs and flour have been mixed in. Then add the milk.

Crêpes "Miriam"

Time: 1¼ hours
Ingredients:
For the crêpes
4 eggs
salt
¾ cup all-purpose flour
½ cup milk
1 tbsp butter or lard
For the filling and sauce
8 oz calf's brain and marrow
4 oz chicken livers, cleaned
1 clove garlic
a handful of parsley, chopped
4 tbsp butter
2 tbsp olive oil
a little dry Marsala
1 tbsp tomato paste, diluted
  with a little water
salt and pepper
3 tbsp flour
2 cups milk, heated
a little nutmeg
1 oz (¼ cup) grated Parmesan
  cheese
1 egg yolk

Prepare and cook the crêpes as described for Priest's housekeeper's crêpes on page 180.

Blanch the brains and marrow in boiling water for a few seconds. Drain and chop together with the chicken livers. Brown the whole clove of garlic and the parsley in 1½ tablespoons of the butter, and the oil. Add the mixed meats and cook over a high heat for a few minutes. Pour on a little Marsala and add the tomato paste and continue simmering for a few minutes. Finally, add salt, pepper and remove from the heat.

Melt the remaining butter in a saucepan and stir in the flour. Mix well to eliminate any lumps. Dilute with the hot milk, poured in a little at a time, and stir constantly. You should obtain a smooth béchamel sauce. Season with salt, pepper and nutmeg. Add the Parmesan and, with the

pan off the heat, the egg yolk.
Preheat the oven to 350°F.
Mix half the béchamel with the meat mixture and place a little in the center of each crêpe. Roll them up and place them side by side in a buttered baking dish. Pour the rest of the béchamel on top and bake in the oven until a gratin topping forms.

Hint: As this is a very rich dish, serve it with light accompaniments such as a tossed green salad.

Crêpes with mushrooms

Time: 1 ¼ hours
Ingredients:
For the crêpes
4 eggs
salt
¾ cup all-purpose flour
½ cup milk
1 tbsp butter or lard
For the filling and sauce
10 oz fresh mushrooms
  (preferably cèpes-wood),
  cleaned and thinly sliced
7 tbsp butter
salt
1 tbsp flour
1 cup milk
a little nutmeg
4 oz ham, chopped

Prepare and cook the crêpes as described for Priest's housekeeper's crêpes on page 180.
Sauté the mushrooms in 2 tablespoons of the butter with a pinch of salt. In another saucepan, melt 2 tablespoons of the butter and stir in the flour.
Dilute with the hot milk, poured in a little at a time, and stir constantly. Season with salt and nutmeg and cook the béchamel sauce for 5 minutes. Remove from the heat and mix in the ham and mushrooms.
Preheat the oven to 350°F.
Place some filling in the center of each crêpe and roll it up. Arrange them in a buttered baking dish and pour on the remaining butter, melted. Bake in the oven for a few minutes.

Hint: To enhance the flavor of the sauce, force a few of the mushrooms through a sieve. You can also use dried cèpes-wood for this sauce (soaked in warm water and then drained).

Gorgonzola crêpes

Time: 1 hour
Ingredients:
For the crêpes
4 eggs
salt
¾ cup all-purpose flour

¹/₂ cup milk
1 tbsp butter or lard
For the filling and sauce
5 tbsp butter
1 tbsp flour
1 cup milk, heated
salt and pepper
a little nutmeg
5 oz mild Gorgonzola cheese,
  cut into pieces
2 oz (¹/₂ cup) grated Parmesan
  cheese

Prepare and cook the crêpes as described for Priest's housekeeper's crêpes on page 180.

Melt 2 tablespoons of the butter in a saucepan and stir in the flour. Dilute with the hot milk, poured in a little at a time, and stir constantly. Season with salt, pepper and nutmeg. Cook the béchamel sauce for 5 minutes. Remove from the heat and stir in the Gorgonzola and half the Parmesan.

Preheat the oven to 350°F.

Spread the mixture on the crêpes and roll them up. Arrange them in a buttered baking dish. Pour on the remaining butter, melted, and sprinkle with the rest of the Parmesan. Bake in the oven for a few minutes.

Hint: A delicate and delicious dish. If you are cooking for children, use grated Swiss cheese instead of Gorgonzola.

Sophisticated crêpes

Time: 1¹/₂ hours
Ingredients:
For the crêpes
4 eggs
salt
³/₄ cup all-purpose flour
¹/₂ cup milk
1 tbsp butter or lard
For the filling and sauce
1 small piece of onion, chopped
5 tbsp butter
8 oz ground pork
8 oz lean ground beef
²/₃ oz dried cèpes-wood
  mushrooms, soaked,
  drained and sliced
salt and pepper
about 1 cup stock, heated
2 tbsp flour
1 small black truffle (optional),
  grated
1 lb mozzarella cheese, chopped
a little nutmeg

Prepare the crêpes as described for Priest's housekeeper's crêpes on page 180.

To make the filling, sauté the onion in 2 tablespoons of the butter and add the ground pork and beef, the mushrooms and a pinch of salt. Simmer, adding 1 to 2 tablespoons of the stock if necessary. Meanwhile, melt 2 tablespoons of the butter in another saucepan and stir in the flour. Mix well and dilute with the boiling stock, poured in a little at a time. Cook the sauce for a few minutes, then stir in a few tablespoons of the meat mixture, a little truffle and the mozzarella; season with salt, pepper and nutmeg. Preheat the oven to 350°F. Fill the crêpes with the filling mixture, roll them up and arrange them in a buttered baking dish. Pour on the remaining sauce and scatter slivers of truffle and butter over the top. Bake in the oven for a few minutes.

Hint: With this main course, serve a mixed raw vegetable salad with a dressing of olive oil, salt and pepper.

Crêpes with asparagus

Time: 1½ hours
Ingredients:
For the crêpes
4 eggs
salt
¾ cup all-purpose flour
½ cup milk
1 tbsp butter or lard
For the filling and sauce
a bunch of asparagus,
  weighing about 2 lb
6 tbsp butter

salt and pepper
¼ cup flour
2 cups milk, heated
a little nutmeg
2 oz (½ cup) grated Parmesan
  cheese
4 oz Gruyère cheese, sliced

Prepare and cook the crêpes as described for Priest's housekeeper's crêpes on page 180.
To make the filling, boil the asparagus (or, preferably, steam it), remove the stalks and the hardest green part and sauté the tips with 2 tablespoons of the butter and a pinch of salt. Then, force through a sieve.
Prepare a fairly thick béchamel sauce by melting the rest of the butter and stirring in the flour and the hot milk. Season with salt, pepper and nutmeg and cook for 5 minutes. Reserve about a quarter of the sauce and mix the asparagus purée with the rest, together with the Parmesan. Preheat the oven to 350°F. Spread the mixture on the crêpes, placing a slice of Gruyère on each. Roll the crêpes up and arrange them in a buttered baking dish. Spread on the rest of the béchamel and bake in the oven for a few minutes.
Hint: Out of season, you can use frozen asparagus tips.

gorgonzola crêpes (p. 182)

SUBJECT INDEX

RECIPE INDEX